How to Play Better Baseball

How to Play
Better Baseball

C. Paul Jackson

Illustrated by Leonard Kessler

Thomas Y. Crowell Company · New York

For Tommy, Ed, Charlie, Bruce, Bob, and Steve Jackson

Contents

1.
FIRST THINGS FIRST

So you are interested in baseball.

Would you like some tips on how to play the game? Do you want to find out some of the things that a fan or an umpire would know?

Fan and *umpire* are probably terms that you already know. Some of the others you will find in this book may possibly be new. Many of them are explained in a list at the back.

Without being too technical, we are going to explain the game and offer tips that may help you to be a better ballplayer.

Baseball is played on vacant lots, in fields, pastures, or in fine parks built especially for the purpose. No matter where the game takes place, there are four things we cannot do without—a ball, a bat, players, and an area large enough to play on.

1

2　　The most simple form of baseball is a game between two players. One player has the ball and the other the bat. Further on in the book you will read about official baseballs, limitations on bats, and things of that sort. For a two-player game any ball may be used, and any piece of wood may serve as bat.

The player with the ball stands at a certain distance from a spot called home base. He is the PITCHER.

The player with the bat stands beside home base. He will stand at the right or left of the base according to whether he bats right-handed or left-handed. He, of course, is the BATTER.

In a two-player game or in sand-lot games, any flat object may be used for home base. The official rules say that home base shall be a five-sided slab of whitened rubber.

Ballplayers usually call the home base "home plate." Sometimes they just call it "the plate."

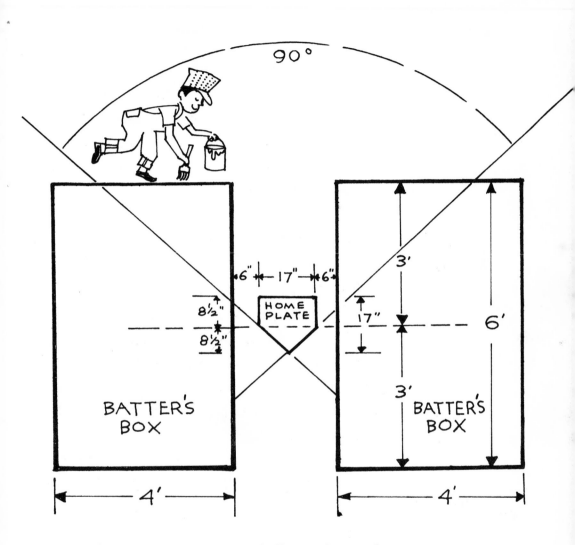

90°

←6"→|←17"→|←6"→

8½"

HOME
PLATE

17"

3'

6'

8½"

3'

BATTER'S
BOX

BATTER'S
BOX

←————4'————→

←————4'————→

Above are the shape and dimensions of
an official home plate.

The pitcher tries to throw the ball so that
the batter cannot hit it well. He must pitch   3

STRIKE ZONE

it into the strike zone. This zone is defined in the official rules. It is the rectangular space above the plate from the batter's knees to his armpits. Since the plate is seventeen inches wide, the strike zone is seventeen inches wide. The height of the zone varies with the height of the batter.

When a pitch is not in the strike zone, it is called a ball. Four balls pitched to a batter give him a base on balls. In other words, he is allowed to take a base with no risk of being put out by the pitcher, or by any other player when there are more than two in the game. Making a put-out, or being put out, will be discussed in more detail later on.

A pitch in the strike zone not hit at by the batter is a strike. It is also a strike if the batter hits the ball foul. Foul balls will be fully explained in another part of the book. The batter may hit any number of foul balls, but they must be made from swinging the bat, or the ball hitting the bat by accident.

4

Sometimes a batter bunts—that is, he jabs the bat out to meet the ball without actually swinging. A batter is not allowed to bunt foul after he has two strikes. If he does, he will be put out.

A batter is permitted three strikes. He is out (becomes a put-out, strikes out) if he does not swing at a pitch in the strike zone after he has had two strikes. He also strikes out if he does swing but fails to hit the ball.

The batter tries to hit the ball far enough so that he can run to bases without being put out. In this simple two-player game a put-out is made if the pitcher can get the batted ball back to the plate before the batter can run to the other base and return to home base. Sometimes the two players change places after every put-out. Sometimes they play without changing until two or three put-outs are made.

This two-player game, frequently played in cities, is sometimes called one o' cat, one eye cat, or one old cat.

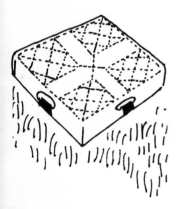

6   Suppose more players join the game. There may be enough so that there are two or three batters. In this case, there will be two or three bases besides home base.

The rules say there shall be a first base, second base, and third base. These bases shall be white canvas bags fifteen inches square. They cannot be less than three inches or more than five inches thick. They shall be filled with soft material and securely fastened to the ground. The diagram of the layout of a baseball field shown in Chapter 2 shows where the bases should be located.

With two or three batters and several players to catch, stop, or chase batted balls, the game becomes what is known as "work-up." One player stands behind the batter, back of home plate. He catches pitches that are not hit. He is the CATCHER.

When a batter makes an out in work-up, the catcher moves up to the batter's position. The pitcher moves to the catcher's position. Another player moves to the

pitcher's place, and every other player 7
moves one step nearer to becoming batter.
Each player tries to get the batter out so
that he can work up to a turn at bat.

When there are enough players to form
sides, the game becomes "scrub." A side
stays at bat until three of its men make
put-outs. Then the sides change. The team
that was in the field comes up to bat; the
side that has batted goes into the field.

TEAM
THAT WAS
IN THE FIELD
COMES UP
TO BAT.

TEAM
AT BAT
GOES
INTO
THE FIELD.

8   There are different ways of making put-outs. A batter makes a put-out when he strikes out. An out is also made when a batted ball is caught before it touches the ground or anything fastened to the ground. If a player in the field catches any batted ball not in the air, he can put the batter out by throwing the ball in time to reach first base before the batter gets there. A base runner becomes a put-out when he is tagged (touched) with the ball before he arrives at a base he is trying to reach. An out occurs when a base runner is forced to try for the next base because a team-mate is entitled to the one he is on, and the ball reaches the advanced base before the runner.

A batter may hit a single. This means that he reaches only first base. He may reach first base if a player tries to field a ball and fumbles, or misses the ball, so that he cannot throw it to the base in time. This is called an error by the fielder.

A batter may hit the ball far enough, or

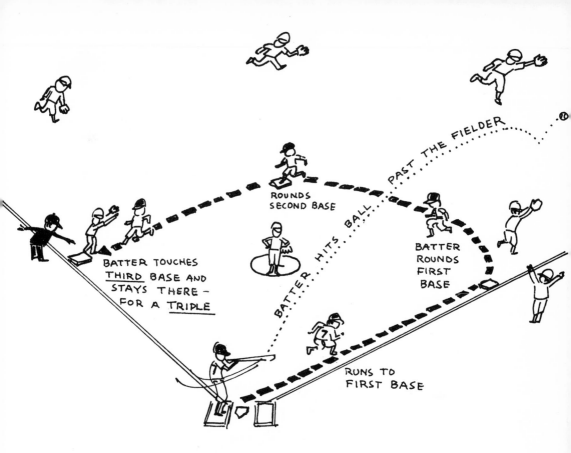

ROUNDS
SECOND BASE

PAST THE FIELDER

BATTER HITS BALL

BATTER TOUCHES
THIRD BASE AND
STAYS THERE –
FOR A TRIPLE

BATTER
ROUNDS
FIRST
BASE

RUNS TO
FIRST BASE

hit it to a spot a fielder cannot reach in time, and get to second base. This is a two-base hit. Players sometimes call it a double. On a ball batted far enough, the batter might reach third base. Such a three-base hit is also known as a triple.

Perhaps sometime when you are batter, you will hit the ball out of the park, or far enough so that you can run all the way 9

10 around the bases without being put out.
You have hit a home run! A homer! You
are a long-ball hitter! A slugger! Teammates will rush to shake your hand as you
cross the plate. For a moment or two you
are Babe Ruth or Roger Maris, or Mickey
Mantle, or any other home-run slugger!

Of course, you know that a game played
according to the Official Baseball Rules
is between teams of nine players each. In
one of these regulation games there are
certain features that never change. Every
player goes to the plate to bat when it is
his turn. Each team tries to make more
runs than the other. The game is set up on
a nine-inning basis, but no matter how
many innings are played, each side must
have the same number of chances to be at
bat. If anything happens to keep a team
from having its final bats, the score returns
to that of the last complete inning.

A run is made when a team succeeds in
getting one of its players around the bases
without being put out. An inning has been

played when each side has been at bat until it has made three outs. If the score is tied at the end of nine innings, extra innings are played. The game goes on until one team has more runs than the other and both have had an equal number of turns at bat.

Have you ever missed a favorite TV show because its time was given up for the telecast of a baseball game? Perhaps it was part of the World Series, held each year at the end of the regular baseball season. At this time the teams which have won the major-league championships play each other. You may have watched telecasts of the All Star game, too. This is the one in which star players chosen from the teams of one league play against stars of the other league.

The major leagues are made up of professional baseball teams representing various large cities. The National League and the American League have been with us for a good many years.

2.
THE PLAYING FIELD

HIGH schools, colleges, recreational leagues, and all professionally organized leagues provide playing areas just for baseball. They are based on an infield of standard measurements which is called a diamond.

The diamond is really a square with sides ninety feet long. It is laid out with home base, marked by the plate of hard white rubber, at its western corner. First base is at the southern corner, second base at the eastern corner, and third base at the northern corner. Of course, a diamond may be laid out so its corners are in other directions.

In your imagination draw a line between first base and third base. Halfway along this line is a rectangle twenty-four inches long and six inches wide. This is the

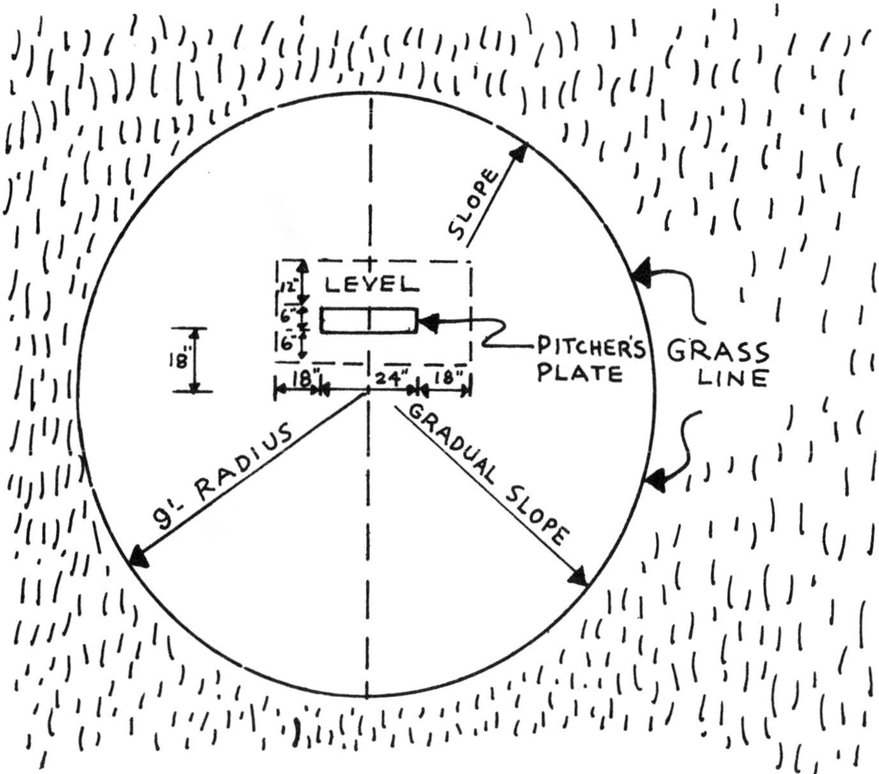

SLOPE

LEVEL

18"

PITCHER'S PLATE

GRASS LINE

18" 24" 18"

9' RADIUS

GRADUAL SLOPE

pitcher's plate. It is usually made of the same hard rubber as home plate. On sports pages it is often called "the rubber" or "the slab." The front edge of the pitcher's rectangle must lie sixty feet and six inches from the back point of home plate. The rubber is fifteen inches higher than home plate. The ground around the rubber slopes gradually downward.

13

14　　Imagine that one end of a nine-foot string is glued to the center of the pitching rubber. Then pretend that you are drawing the other end of the string around the pitcher's plate in a big circle. This is the sloping area.

SIDE VIEW OF "MOUND"

It is no wonder that the pitcher's box is sometimes called the "mound" or "hill." It is easy to understand, too, why a pitcher who is hit hard enough to be removed from the game is said to be "knocked off the hill," "shelled off the mound," or "batted out of the box."

Beginning at the back point of home plate, a line is drawn past first base and all the way to the outfield fence or to the facing of the stands (if there are stands). Another line like this runs from home plate, past third base, and on to the fence or to the facing of the stands. These are the foul lines. They are usually made with

powdered chalk or the kind of lime that   15
does not burn flesh or grass.

From first base to second base, and from
second base to third base there are only
imaginary lines.

That part of the ballfield between the
real foul lines and the imaginary lines that
complete the diamond is the infield. The
portion of the ballfield outside the diamond
is the outfield.

A ball batted into the air beyond the infield must stay between the foul lines to be
a fair ball. A ball batted onto the ground
must stay between the foul lines going past
first base or third base to be a fair ball.

FLY BALL
FAIR BALL

GROUND BALL
FAIR
BALL

FOUL
BALL

FOUL LINE

GROUND
BALL·· FAIR
BALL

FLY BALL
FAIR BALL

FOUL
BALL

FOUL
LINE

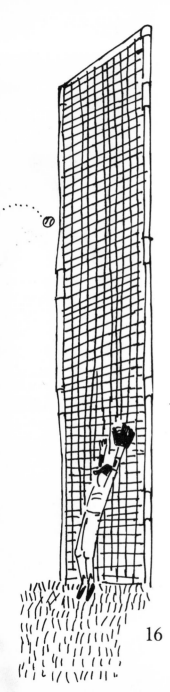

Only fair balls permit the batter to become a base runner. Men already on base can advance only on fair balls. An exception to this rule occurs when a foul ball batted into the air is caught. In this case, a base runner may advance at his own risk. A foul ball hit into the air and caught before touching the ground causes the batter to be out.

The distance from home plate along the foul lines to the fence or stands is not always the same. It varies according to how much space there is.

When fences are too close to home plate, one way in which the problem is solved is to erect a tall screen. This is what the Los Angeles Dodgers did in Memorial Coliseum. The other way is for the two teams to agree to ground rules before playing. The ground rule may limit a batter who hits the ball over the low fence to two bases.

The diagram in the Official Baseball Rules shows a grass line in two places. One marks the circular area of outfield

16

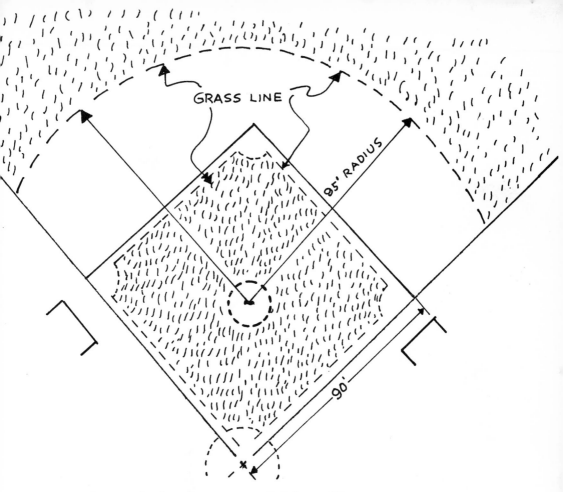

GRASS LINE

95' RADIUS

90'

grass beyond the bare—or "skinned"—
base paths. This grass line is an arc drawn
from foul line to foul line with a radius
of ninety-five feet from the center of the
pitcher's rubber. The other grass line forms
a circle around the pitcher's mound at a
distance of nine feet from the center of the
rubber.

17

18   Professional-league ball parks and most college ballfields have grass infields with bare base paths and pitcher's mound. Plenty of other diamonds are laid out in areas where there is no grass. Nothing in the rules forbids it.

Many big-league stars have given young players the same advice: Treasure your arm. Never throw too hard or try to throw too fast for your size and age. Muscles that are not fully developed should not be subjected to the strain of overthrowing.

There just is no way to cure an arm that is too badly strained. Even if you don't hurt your arm, you still should not try to throw too far or too hard while you are growing. You may acquire poor throwing habits.

Most leagues for players twelve and under scale down dimensions for playing fields. Here is a diagram of a baseball field scaled down to two-thirds regular size. This size is best for players under thirteen. For players a little older, perhaps a field scaled to three-fourths size might be better.

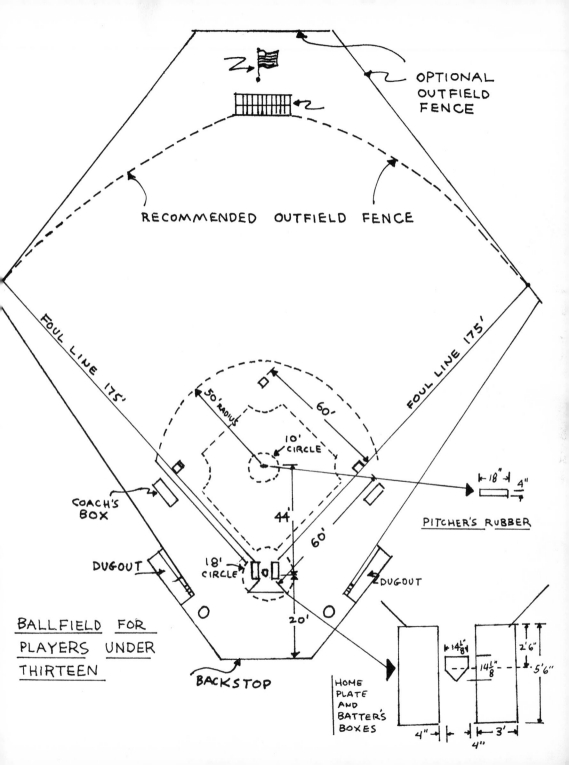

OPTIONAL OUTFIELD FENCE

RECOMMENDED OUTFIELD FENCE

FOUL LINE 175'

FOUL LINE 175'

50' RADIUS

60'

10' CIRCLE

44'

60'

COACH'S BOX

18' CIRCLE

DUGOUT

DUGOUT

20'

18"

4"

PITCHER'S RUBBER

BALLFIELD FOR PLAYERS UNDER THIRTEEN

BACKSTOP

HOME PLATE AND BATTER'S BOXES

14 1/8"

14 1/8"

2'6"

5'6"

4"

4"

3'

3.
EQUIPMENT

THE uniforms of baseball players must follow regulations of the Official Baseball Rules. All players on a team wear uniforms exactly alike in color, trim, and style. Any part of an undershirt that is exposed must be of the same color for all players on that team. A player whose uniform differs from those of his teammates will not be allowed to play in a game.

The club insignia, the numbers, and the letters may be a different color from that of the uniform itself. Aside from these, no material of another color may be sewn onto it. Nothing that imitates or suggests the shape of a baseball may be part of a uniform. No glass buttons or any shiny metal may be used. Reflections from the sun, or from lights in a night game, might flash before a batter's eyes! A player must not attach anything to his shoe other than the ordinary shoe plate or toe plate.

Such are the strict requirements of the official rules. In a sand-lot game you can play just as good baseball without any uniform at all.

As for equipment other than uniforms, what do the rules tell us about that?

The official baseball has a core of cork, rubber, or similar material, with yarn wound around and around it. The outside is made of two pieces of white horsehide stitched tightly together. The ball must weigh between five and five and one-fourth ounces. It must not measure less than nine inches or more than nine and one-fourth inches around.

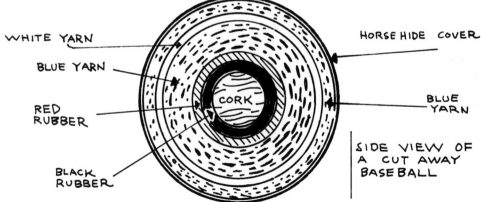

WHITE YARN

BLUE YARN

RED RUBBER

BLACK RUBBER

CORK

HORSE HIDE COVER

BLUE YARN

SIDE VIEW OF A CUT AWAY BASEBALL

22   When you hold a baseball in your hand you can feel the seam made by the slanted stitches holding the pieces of leather together. The raised seam is a great help to a pitcher gripping the ball for a fast one, a curve, a slider, sinker, change-up, or knuckler. These are pitches you will hear more about in Chapter 9.

The baseball bat must be made of wood, the rule book says. Pieces of wood cemented together may be used, or the bat may be one solid piece. No matter which type it is, the pieces of wood must all have the grain running the length of the bat. Most bats are made from one piece of solid and well-seasoned wood.

The bat must be smooth and round, with no flat surface area. At the thickest part it must not measure more than two and three-fourths inches. In length it must not be more than forty-two inches. The handle end of the bat may be roughened or wrapped with tape or twine for as much as eighteen inches.

There is no rule regarding the weight.

For the beginning ballplayer the best bat is the one that fits him. Never settle on a bat simply because it is the model used by some famous big-league hitter. His size and needs are different from yours.

When it comes to the catcher of a team, the rule book is generous. Here are the items he is allowed to wear: a leather glove or mitt of any size, shape, or weight; shin guards, mask, and chest protector.

A catcher can certainly use these. In his position behind the batter, he must catch balls pitched as fast as his pitcher can throw. Sometimes he must stop foul tips (balls merely tipped by the bat when it is swung), which come back very fast. Or

MASK

GLOVE

CHEST
PROTECTOR

SHIN
GUARDS

suppose a player on the other team is trying to reach home base. He often slides, feet forward, with the metal cleats on the bottoms of his shoes exposed. The catcher's job is to block him. This is another time when he really needs his special equipment.

The man at first base must catch balls thrown hard to him by other players. One of his most important jobs is to catch such throws and touch first base before the player who hit the ball gets there. The rules permit the first baseman to wear a leather glove or mitt not more than twelve inches long from top to bottom. It cannot be more than eight inches wide across the palm, from the base of the thumb crotch to the outer edge of the mitt.

At times some first basemen have tried to use mitts which were more like butterfly nets. For this reason there are restrictions on the size, shape, web, and depth of pocket of a first baseman's mitt. You can find these, if you are interested, in Rule 1.13 of the Official Baseball Rules.

Each fielder other than first baseman or catcher may wear a leather glove. From the base of the thumb crotch to the outer edge, the glove must not be more than twelve inches long or more than eight inches wide, but it may be of any weight. The webbing between thumb and fingers may not be made of wound or wrapped lacing to form a net or trap-type mitt. Ballplayers sometimes refer to the fielder's glove as a finger mitt.

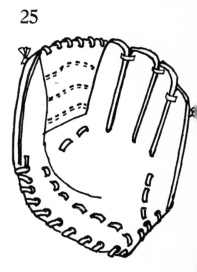

The pitcher's glove must be all one color, the rules tell us, but must not be white or gray. No foreign material may be fastened to it.

There are good reasons for all these rules. For example, in 1946 a United States Army timing device tested fast balls pitched by Bob Feller, one of baseball's great speed-ball pitchers. His fast ball was clocked at 146 feet per second at the pitching distance of sixty feet six inches. This works out to a speed of ninety-nine and a half miles per hour. At that speed a batter

26 just cannot have his vision distracted by anything!

Sliding pads to protect the hips are not required by the rules but most players wear these under their uniforms. They help prevent strawberries—the red spots left when skin is scraped off in making a slide.

You probably know the term *spikes*—the name ballplayers have given to their shoes because of the triangular metal plates or cleats on the soles. The shoes are made of soft lightweight leather, sometimes of kangaroo skin. Baseball can be played without spikes but they will make it easier for you to stop quickly and help keep you from slipping. A real ballplayer, of course, will use his spikes properly. It is never his purpose to come onto a base in such a way as to injure an opponent.

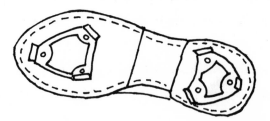

4.
A MAKE-BELIEVE INNING

Now let's say that we have a place to play, a baseball, and a bat. Or perhaps there will be several bats, since each player needs one that fits him. We have a pitcher's rubber, a home plate, canvas bags for the other bases, and two teams of nine boys each.

First of all, everybody should take part in a warming-up session. It is foolish ever to throw hard until you have loosened your muscles properly. Otherwise you may ruin your arm.

While the players are warming up we can see about lineup and batting order. A little has already been said about the pitcher, catcher, and first baseman. Later on there will be more about what the individual players do at each of the nine positions on a team. For the time being, it will

28 be enough to know only the following things.

Just as the first baseman takes throws made to first base, the second baseman takes throws to second base, and the third baseman takes throws to third.

The shortstop protects the area between second base and the third baseman's territory. He also takes throws made to second base when the second baseman is not near enough to cover it himself.

The first baseman, second baseman, third baseman, and shortstop are the infielders. Their job is to keep balls batted into their territory from becoming base hits. Such a hit occurs when a batter hits a ball that cannot be reached in time to throw him out at first base.

An infielder tries to catch any ball batted in the air that he can reach. He fields a ball batted into the territory by catching, stopping, or scooping it up in his glove. Although they always try, infielders often cannot reach the ball in time.

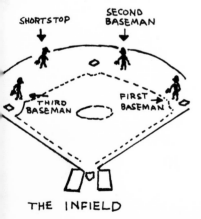

THE INFIELD

The outfield is made up of three positions: left field, center field, and right field. The left fielder covers left field, of course. It is his job to field balls batted on the ground (grounders) when they get past third baseman and shortstop. He is also expected to catch any fly ball he can reach when it is batted into his territory. This includes about one third of the outfield, moving toward the center, as well as any area he can get to outside the left foul line. 29

The center fielder patrols the center third of the outfield. He must catch balls batted into the air in this area. It is also his duty to field grounders that are hit past the shortstop and second baseman into his territory.

Right field is the third of the outfield from center field to the right foul line. A right fielder tries to catch the ball in the air if it is a fly, either in fair ground or foul territory outside the foul line. Another part of his job is to field grounders that get past the first baseman or second baseman and into the field.

No matter what position a player may have in the field, when his team is at bat he has a definite place in the batting order. This is decided before the game and cannot be changed. Whether or not a player is taken from the game, or moved to another position, his place in the batting order remains the same. Any substitute for him must bat in that same place. You can easily see how unfair it would be for teams to move their best batters around and send them to the plate whenever they choose.

All right, everybody has warmed up. Let's see about starting the game.

We have someone to be umpire. He will decide whether pitches are in the strike zone and are strikes, or are outside the strike zone and are balls. He will say when men are safe on plays at the bases and when they are out. And he will decide whether a batted ball is fair or foul. A baseball game can be played without an umpire. It goes much more smoothly, however, with an umpire, rather than the players, making the decisions.

"Play ball!" the umpire calls. "Batter up!"

The leadoff man in the batting order of the team at bat takes his place at the plate. The pitcher is ready. He delivers the first pitch of the game. It is in the strike zone but our batter stands without swinging at it.

"Strike one!" cries the umpire.

The second pitch is too low and once

again the batter fails to swing. "Ball one!" the umpire shouts.

Now, here comes the third pitch. Let's see what our batter will do this time. He swings a little too soon. The ball skitters over the ground outside the foul line as it passes third base.

"Foul ball! Strike two!"

(Remember that a foul ball counts as a strike when the batter has less than two strikes.)

The count is now one and two. This means one ball and two strikes. In calling the count on a batter, the number of strikes is always given last.

The leadoff man swings mightily at the next pitch. His bat connects with nothing but thin air.

"Strike three! A strike-out! One out!"

The second batter swings at the first pitch made to him. The ball is in the air, to the left side of the diamond. It is too far out to be reached by an infielder. Yet it is

32 not hit deeply enough to be caught by an

outfielder. The ball drops safely and the batter reaches first base. Now his aim is to get all the way around the bases and score a run.

"We'll score a million runs! Get in there and sock another hit!" Cries of encouragement to the next batter come from his mates on the bench, or wherever they are waiting.

This batter takes a strike, then a ball, and another ball. A second strike is called by the umpire. Then he calls a third ball. If the pitcher doesn't get the next pitch in the strike zone, the batter will be allowed to go to first base.

The pitch is wide.

"Ball four!" The umpire motions the batter to first base. At the same time the runner on first moves along to second. Since this is a base on balls no one can tag him out.

Now we have runners on first and second base and only one out. A good hit will score a run. With a long hit, for more than a single, both base runners may score. **33**

34 This is an exciting point in the game. The catcher walks out to the middle of the diamond to talk to the pitcher. Then one of the infielders hurries over to the mound. They want to be sure that the pitcher is not upset. Encouraging shouts from his other teammates ring in the pitcher's ears.

"Buzz that ball in there, kid! . . . Whiz that rock past him! . . . Nothing to worry about, you can get 'em out of there! . . . Give those guys the old bench pitch! . . . Make 'em hit to get on! . . . Somebody'll go get it! . . . We'll get the two for you!"

The catcher jogs back behind the plate and crouches. He gives the pitcher a sign and holds his mitt for a target. The signs (signals) have been decided on beforehand by the two of them. Those most often used by catchers are one finger against the mitt for a fast ball, and two fingers for a curve.

This time the sign is for a fast ball. When the pitch proves to be in the strike zone, the batter hits it sharply. A swift grounder skips a little to the shortstop's right. He fields the ball and tosses it to the second baseman, who has run over to the bag.

The second baseman kicks second base before the runner from first arrives, and this man is forced out. Throwing hard and quickly, the second baseman smacks the ball into the first baseman's mitt an instant before the runner's spikes hit the first base bag. Now the batter is out too.

Ballplayers say the infield "got the two." In other words, two put-outs have been made in a double play.

Now there are three outs, so the two teams change sides.

In every baseball game, even if both teams are from the same town, one is always considered the visiting team. This is the one that opens the game at bat. When the visiting team has made three outs, the home team comes to bat. In the final inning of a game the home team is at an advantage in having the last bats.

You have probably heard the terms "top of an inning" and "bottom of an inning." There is a reason for these, as for everything else. In keeping score, the top of the scorecard is used for the visiting team. The score of the home team is put at the bottom. Sometimes the bottom of an inning is spoken of as the "last of an inning."

In our imaginary game we are now at the bottom of the first inning. The first batter at the plate at the start of any half

LEFT FIELDER CATCHES
LINE DRIVE ... OUT NUMBER ONE

inning is called the leadoff man. Our
present leadoff man swings at the very
first pitch, hits the ball well, and makes
a line drive. Unfortunately for him, the
ball goes straight to the left fielder, who
catches it, face-high. This is one put-out
for the home team.

Next, the man who is second in this
team's batting order comes to the plate.
He is a left-handed batter. He does not
like pitches that curve, and the pitcher
knows it. The first pitch is a curve that
catches the outside corner of the plate in
the strike zone.

The umpire calls, "Strike one!"   37

The second pitch is a curve that bends too wide to be in the strike zone. It is a ball, the umpire decides.

A third pitch curves over the outer edge of the plate. It is within the strike zone, waist high.

"One ball and two strikes!"

Now the batter crowds closer to the plate. He must swing at any pitch in the strike zone even though it is a curve.

But the pitcher does not throw a curve. He tries to catch the batter off balance with a pitch just over the inside edge of the plate. The pitch is thrown too far inside. The ball nicks the batter's arm. A batter hit by a pitched ball goes to first base so now there is a base runner on first.

The third batter is a very fast runner. He is also a fine bunter. A bunt, you remember, is made when a player taps the ball with a loosely held bat instead of swinging at it. When this happens, the ball usually dribbles slowly over the ground. It must go between the foul lines. A good

bunter who is a swift runner can often
beat out a bunt. Even if he should be
thrown out at first base, the runner on first
would be advanced to second. In a case like
this it would be a sacrifice bunt.

This batter bunts the first pitch. Slowly
the ball dribbles between the mound and
first base. The pitcher starts for the ball but
the first baseman charges in and grabs it.

The second baseman runs to cover the
bag. The hurried throw from the first baseman does not arrive until after the bunter
has crossed the bag, however. Now there
are base runners on second and first. There
is one out.

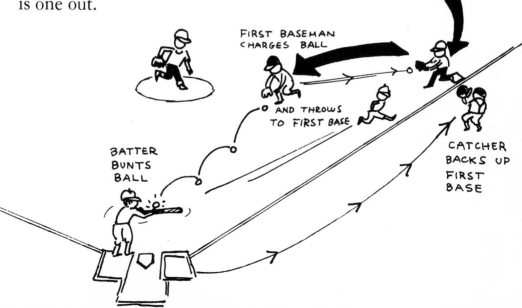

SECOND BASEMAN
COVERS FIRST
BASE

FIRST BASEMAN
CHARGES BALL

AND THROWS
TO FIRST BASE

BATTER
BUNTS
BALL

CATCHER
BACKS UP
FIRST
BASE

The fourth batter swings hard and misses. Then he swings at another pitch and misses. At his third swing, a long high fly ball rises into the sky.

After caught fly balls, base runners may advance at the risk of being thrown out. The fielder is so deep when he catches this fly that the base runners each tag up (stand with one foot touching the base) and advance a base as soon as the catch is made. Now there are baserunners on second and third.

A safe hit would probably score both runners, so the pitcher is eager to fool the next batter. Cleverly he tricks the man at the plate into swinging at a pitch that looks waist high. As the ball comes into the strike zone, it dips in what is known as a sinker curve. There will be more about these in the chapter on pitching, Chapter 9.

The batter tops the sinker curve, and, in one long hop, the ball goes straight into the pitcher's glove. This is an easy put-out at first base. Again the teams change sides.

5.
PLAYING FIRST BASE

THE first baseman usually handles the ball more often in a game than any other fielder on the whole team. He has three main jobs:

1. Field those balls hit into his area that he can reach.

2. Take throws from the pitcher, the catcher, infielders, and outfielders.

3. Work closely with the pitcher and catcher to hold base runners on first base close to the bag.

A base runner on first base edges as far toward second as he can. He wants to shorten the distance he will need to run. He may try to "steal," or run to, second base while a pitch is being made. It is called "stealing" the base because it does not require a hit or a base on balls by the batter to get there. If a base runner is

41

42 allowed to lead off too far from the bag, the catcher has little chance of throwing him out.

What makes an ideal first baseman? We asked this question of a man who had played and managed in every classification of organized baseball from Class D to the major leagues. This was his answer: "A tall long-armed guy who throws left-handed. He would have hands as big as hams. They would be as sticky as flypaper when it came to grabbing a baseball. He would be as quick and agile as a monkey. His footwork would be as smooth as a dancing master's. He would be a batter with power to produce the long ball for me."

You can easily see what an advantage it is to be left-handed when you are playing first base. A first baseman's throwing plays are almost always to his right side, to second and third base. They are often split-second plays. A left-handed first baseman can simply draw back his arm and fire the ball. Not having to pivot for the throw can mean the difference between a put-out or the runner's being safe.

Don't be discouraged if you don't measure up to the ideal. Many first basemen are right-handed throwers. Many are not tall. If you can catch a ball well and present a good target, you can make yourself into a good first baseman.

To present a good target you have to get near the bag and give the thrower something at which to aim. Your body, your outstretched arms, and your mitt all enter into this. If your teammates have confidence that you will gobble up a poor throw, this also helps your ability to present a good target.

44   Above all, a first baseman must learn correct footwork. He must be able to step quickly to either side of the bag for wide throws.

When an infielder grabs a batted ball he rarely has time for careful aim of his throw to first base. The first baseman must expect some throws wide to one side or the other, high, in the dirt. A good first baseman practices until he snags them all automatically.

There are three things always to keep in mind:

1. You *must* catch the ball. You can do a split that a professional dancer might envy; you can stretch so gracefully that you make motion into poetry—but these mean nothing if you let the ball go through, under, over, or past you.

2. You must stretch as far as possible toward the thrower. The split second you save by stretching may get the ball into your mitt just in time to beat the base runner.

3. You must make contact with the bag when you catch the ball. You can't stand on the bag, always, but you must be in such a position that you can stab it with one foot or the other, before the base runner touches it.

Some throws will pull you off the bag. You lunge, dive or sprawl to tag the runner before he can touch the base. Whether done gracefully or by scrambling, any play you make that gets the base runner out is a good play.

Your catcher fields a bunt. The ball is between the foul lines or he has no play. You stand on the side of the bag that is inside the foul line. The catcher throws well inside the line. There is less risk of hitting the base runner.

The runner is entitled to three feet as a base path and is no doubt barreling down the line. If the catcher must throw straight down or across the line because his first baseman is out of position, his peg may hit the runner and you will lose a put-out.

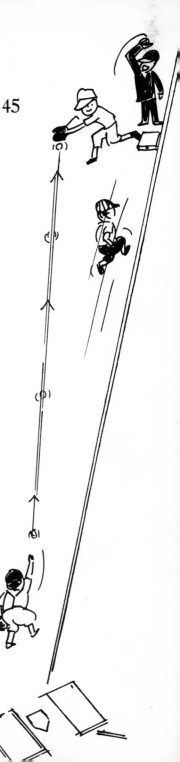

Your catcher drops a third strike. The rules give the batter the right to run on a dropped third strike. The catcher must get the ball to first base ahead of the batter.

Now you step well outside the foul line and hold your mitt out as a target for the catcher. There is less risk of hitting the runner. You catch the ball with less risk of having to lunge in front of the runner charging toward the base.

Watch a first baseman and pitcher when the baseman fields a ground hit ball and the pitcher covers the bag. Properly executed, this is one of the fine plays in baseball. It takes perfect co-operation and timing. Ball and pitcher must get together an instant before the pitcher's foot stabs the bag.

Good timing is seldom accidental. The beautiful timing you see in a game has come from hours of practice by the pitcher and first baseman.

Earlier in the chapter we said that the first baseman holds the base runner close

to the bag. How to do it? With one foot
anchored to the bag? Where to play? Behind the runner? These are questions the
first baseman must answer.

For the most part, he follows a simple
rule. If there is no runner on second, he
holds the man on first by playing on the
bag. When there is a runner on second
base, it is less likely that a steal will be
tried. (In this case it would be a double
steal with both runners advancing.) The
first baseman stays behind the runner and
is in a better position for fielding the ball,
should it be hit his way.

Wherever he plays, the first baseman

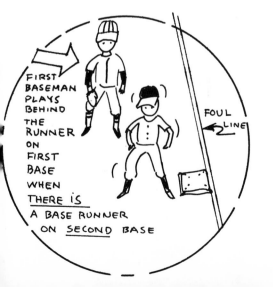

IF THERE IS
NO RUNNER ON
SECOND BASE,
FIRST BASEMAN
PLAYS HERE

FIRST
BASEMAN
PLAYS
BEHIND
THE
RUNNER
ON
FIRST
BASE
WHEN
THERE IS
A BASE RUNNER
ON SECOND BASE

FOUL
LINE

FOUL LINE

48 must always be alert for a quick throw from pitcher or catcher when there is a runner on first base.

BRIEF TIPS FOR FIRST BASEMEN

MAKE A TARGET FOR THE THROWER

1. Make a target for the thrower.
2. Know what you will do with the ball if it is hit to you.
3. Be ready to make a throw anywhere after catching the ball. Be alert.
4. Practice an underhand snap throw to use when you field a ball and there is little time to cut down a runner. (A snap of the wrist at the release of the ball, rather than arm-and-shoulder momentum, supplies the power to the underhand throw.)
5. Study the batters. Play closer to the bag or farther toward second according to where batters most often hit.
6. Learn to shift your feet to take throws near the bag. Have throws purposely thrown wide to you in practice so that you can perfect your footwork.

6.
PLAYING SECOND BASE

THE ball is handled by the second base-man when it is thrown to him as he covers the bag. If he can field (catch or stop) balls batted into his territory, either on the ground or in the air, he handles those too. His territory is the area from the first baseman's territory to second base. He goes into short right field and across the foul line after short fly balls.

The second baseman is the pivot man— the man in the middle—on double plays started by the third baseman or shortstop.

SECOND BASEMAN

50   We have said that a double play means putting two base runners out in one continuous play. One of these double plays can pull a pitcher out of trouble when there are men on base and none out or only one out. A double play often kills a threatened batting rally. Pitchers have greater confidence when they know the second baseman and shortstop on their team are expert double-play makers.

The double play is most often made with a runner on first and the batter hitting a ball on the ground.

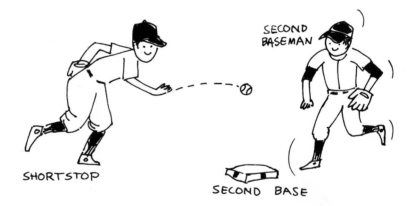

SHORTSTOP

SECOND BASEMAN

SECOND BASE

Let's say that the shortstop fields a grounder and quickly throws it to second base. The second baseman does not stand on the bag all the time, of course. But he runs swiftly toward the base when he sees where the ball is hit. He catches the ball. He steps on the bag to force out the runner from first. He then throws the ball as hard and as quickly as he can to the first base-man to beat the batter who is racing for the first-base bag.

52   If the third baseman—or pitcher—fields the batted ball, it is still the second baseman who makes the force play at second and hurries a throw off to first. A force play happens when a base runner is forced to leave his base because the batter, or runner behind him, is entitled to the advanced base. If he doesn't reach the next base before the ball, he becomes a "force out," the victim of a force play.

Anyone who plays baseball must be able to throw. But the second baseman must be

"FORCE OUT"
AT
SECOND BASE

THIRD BASEMAN
THROWS
TO SECOND BASEMAN

SECOND
BASEMAN
TAGS BAG

RUNNER
FROM FIRST
BASE IS
"FORCED OUT"
AT
SECOND

GROUND BALL IS FIELDED
BY THIRD BASEMAN

able to throw from any position. He may
have to throw while running at top speed.
He may be flat on his face after making
a diving stop. A runner who is coming
into second on a double-play try will make
things as tough for the second baseman
as he can. The second baseman may be
bowled over. He has to be able to make
the throw while falling or even after being
knocked down. Of course, he has to be
able to throw the ball where he wants it
to go.

The second baseman makes most throws
to his left side. You can see that it is an
advantage for a second baseman to throw
right-handed. There is no rule against a
left-handed thrower playing second base.
But for all practical purposes he should
throw right-handed.

We have said that base runners on first
sometimes try to steal second. At a time
like this the second baseman shares with
the shortstop the job of taking the throw
from the catcher. Whichever takes the

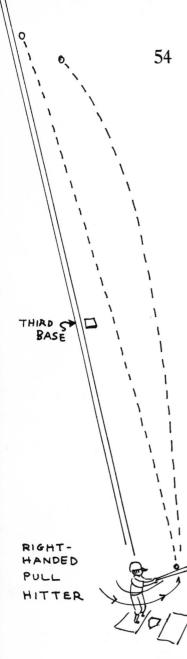

THIRD
BASE

RIGHT-
HANDED
PULL
HITTER

54 throw tries to tag the runner with the ball before he can touch the base. Ballplayers say they "put the tag" or "put the ball" on the runner.

Sometimes the catcher's throw will be high or wide. The first duty of the man taking the throw is to catch or block the ball. He must make sure that the base runner does not get an extra base—run to third—should the throw be bad.

The second baseman plays toward the first-base side of second base. How far over does he play? It depends on several things.

A smart second baseman studies the batters. Perhaps a certain batter often swings late. Such a batter is likely to hit the ball to the opposite field—ballplayers

say the "wrong field." This means that a
right-handed batter who swings toward
left field and normally hits most often to
that field, might hit the ball toward right
field. The reverse would be true with a left-
handed batter.

Some batters pull the ball sharply. This
means that they swing a little too quickly
and their bat connects with the ball in front
of the plate. Their batted balls are likely to
go in the direction of the swing. A right-
handed pull hitter knocks the ball toward
left field. The left-handed pull batter hits
toward right field.

The second baseman remembers whether
the batter swings late or pulls the ball. He
moves to the right or left according to the
batter.

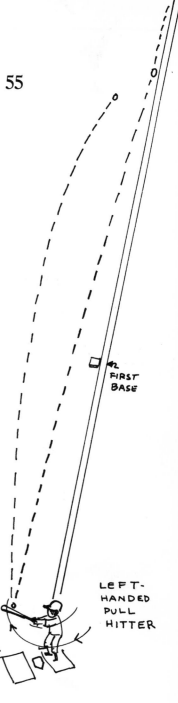

FIRST BASE

LEFT-HANDED PULL HITTER

Second baseman and shortstop work closely together. By means of signals they let each other know which man is going to take the throw—if one is made—when a base runner is on first. A common way of signaling is for the player to hold his glove in front of his face. Only his teammate can see his mouth. An open mouth means "I'll take the throw." A closed mouth means "You take the throw."

In sand-lot baseball the second baseman and shortstop often follow one simple rule. If the batter swings left-handed, the shortstop takes the throw and the second baseman stays in his position. A left-handed batter is more likely to hit into the second baseman's territory. A right-handed batter is more likely to hit into the shortstop's area. The second baseman takes the throw when a right-handed batter is up.

Batters in professional baseball often become skilled at hitting the ball where they want it to go. The second baseman and shortstop try to anticipate—guess, really —which way the batter will try to hit. According to what they decide, one of them stays put to field the ball. With the pitcher's delivery, the other dashes to the bag, ready to take the throw if one is made.

We have said that on many double plays the second baseman is the pivot man. Many second basemen prefer to catch the ball thrown them as their right foot comes down on the bag. Then they pivot (turn), step toward first, and cut loose the throw. A fraction of a second may be saved. It can be the difference between out and safe at first base. But the second baseman is in

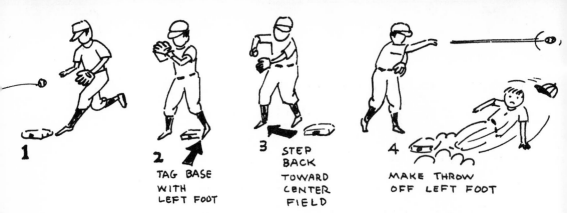

1

2
TAG BASE
WITH
LEFT FOOT

3 STEP
BACK
TOWARD
CENTER
FIELD

4 MAKE THROW
OFF LEFT FOOT

position to be upset by the base runner from first and he may have his throw ruined.

Some second basemen choose to stab the bag with the left foot. Then they make the pivot away from the bag toward center field. The throw is made off the left foot.

You must find out which is best for you by experimenting. The idea is to get the throw safely off to first base in time to complete the double play.

Practice making the double play again and again and again. What the manager said of first basemen goes for second basemen too. They need the quickness and agility of a monkey combined with the smooth footwork of a dancing master.

BRIEF TIPS FOR SECOND BASEMEN

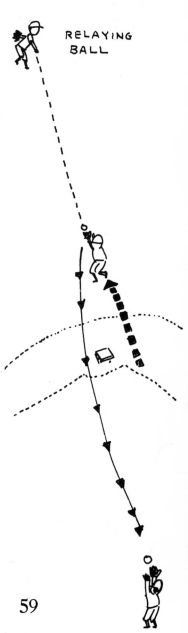

RELAYING BALL

1. Keep your feet behind the bag when tagging.
2. Take enough time in fielding a ground ball to be sure you have it. Except with very slowly hit balls, you never need hurry the throw to first base.
3. Back up second base when the short-stop takes the throw. Back up first base when a catcher drops a third strike.
4. Chase a base runner caught between bases back toward the bag from which he came. Fake throws and make feints (pretended moves).
5. Go out in the field to help relay the ball when a hit is to deep right field or center field. This means you will take the throw from the outfielder and speed the play with a throw of your own. Know to what base you should relay the ball.
6. Be ready to take the throw at first base when the first baseman charges in to field a bunt.

59

7.
PLAYING SHORTSTOP

THE ball comes to the shortstop when he takes throws to second base, when batted balls are hit into his territory, and sometimes when he takes throws at third. The shortstop is responsible for the area between second base and the third baseman's territory.

Between the shortstop's territory and that of the third baseman there is a nasty narrow strip. It is very hard to field balls hit here in time to throw the hitter out at first base. Ballplayers refer to this nasty spot as "the hole."

The shortstop ranges wide to his right
after balls hit into the hole. He races far
to his left to grab grounders over—or even
to the right of—second base. He sometimes
chases fly balls into foul ground beyond
the left foul line. A shortstop normally has
more chances of handling the ball than a
second baseman. He is expected to protect
more territory.

Speed of foot is a great asset in a shortstop. He *must* have quickness and sureness
of hand. He needs a stronger arm than the
second baseman. Scouts for professional
baseball clubs look for two things in a
young player—swiftness of foot and a
strong arm. The two are perhaps needed
more for playing shortstop than for any
other position.

If you do not throw right-handed you
had better forget about playing shortstop.
A left-handed thrower would be at a great
disadvantage.

The shortstop and second baseman must
work smoothly together. They need to be

62 equally adept at starting the double play. As pivot men in the double play they should be equally fast and smooth.

When the shortstop is the middle man in a double play his job may be a little more simple. He will be going toward the base to take the throw. It is not necessary to make a stop or pivot before he throws.

The shortstop should take the ball thrown to him one stride in front of the base. With his left foot he hits the bag. He uses the base to push himself off toward the pitcher's mound. As he lands on his right foot, out of the path of a charging base runner, he throws to first base.

SHORTSTOP
AS MIDDLE
MAN IN
DOUBLE PLAY

TAKES
THROW
FROM
SECOND
BASEMAN

HITS BAG
WITH LEFT FOOT

USE BASE
TO PUSH
OFF TOWARD
MOUND

LAND ON
RIGHT FOOT
AND
THROW TO
FIRST...

Sometimes the throw from the first base- man or second baseman is on the outfield side of the base path. The shortstop may drag his right foot against the corner of the bag. Then he will step wide toward right field and make his throw to first.

Another way is to hit the bag with his left foot and step across the sack to throw off his right foot. Some shortstops think this is the best way. Others favor the drag method just described. The drag is probably harder to learn but it does help avoid collision with the base runner.

64   Holding runners close to the bag is another duty shared by shortstop and second baseman. A pitcher's throw to second—before pitching to the batter—seldom gets the runner out. It may be useful just the same. A runner allowed to take a big lead can sometimes score on a weak hit. To keep him close to the bag, the shortstop or second baseman feints dashes toward it. The closer the man is kept to second, the farther he must run when he does go. The extra distance may cause him to be thrown out.

The shortstop is in the best position to direct his team's defensive play. Often a ball is hit into the air where more than one player could make the catch. The shortstop should call out, telling which man is to make the play. If it is a ball that he can reach himself, the shortstop shouts so that his teammates know he is going to make the play.

The shortstop runs into left field or center field to relay throws from outfielders on

deep hits. He acts as relay man for throws
to third base, to home plate, or to second
base.

The shortstop must take care of second
base on plays in which the second baseman
goes into the outfield to take a relay throw.
The shortstop backs up second base on
plays in which the second baseman takes
throws to the bag.

All infielders should know the infield-
fly rule. It is in the rule book. An infield
fly is a fair ball which is hit into the air
and can be caught by an infielder with
ordinary effort. Say that first and second
base, or first, second, and third base are
occupied and there are fewer than two
outs. Base runners are not forced to run
when an infield fly is declared.

UMPIRE
QUICKLY CALLS
"INFIELD FLY
RULE "
BATTER IS
AUTOMATICALLY
OUT !

66   This is the way the infield fly rule works. The batter is automatically out the instant the umpire calls the hit ball an infield fly. He calls as quickly as possible. But the ball is not dead. It is still in play. Runners are protected against being forced to run. They may advance at the risk of the ball's being caught. If they do run, they may be put out by a throw to the base that they have left before they can get back and touch it.

Base runners will rarely be so foolhardy as to try to advance. Should they do so, the shortstop may be in the best position to call to his teammates and tell them where the throw should be made.

Now and then a shortstop will field a grounder and find a runner trapped between second and third base. Usually the runner stands waiting to see what the shortstop will do. Baseball people say that the runner is "in a hot box" or a "rundown."

When this happens, the shortstop should hang onto the ball and charge toward the

SHORTSTOP

RUNNER CAUGHT
"IN A HOT BOX"

SECOND
BASEMAN

runner. The runner will have to make a break. It is easy for the shortstop to throw the ball and head him off. The shortstop follows his throw in behind the runner. This keeps him in position for a return throw should the runner reverse and try to get back to second base.

Although a runner sometimes makes it safely to base, ballplayers think there is no excuse for letting him escape from a hot box.

A man who has worked with young ballplayers for many years summed up the qualities a shortstop needs. "More than any other player, he must be quick. Speed

SECOND BASE

TERRITORY COVERED BY
SHORTSTOP FOR
POP FLIES

LEFT FIELD
FOUL LINE

of foot makes him that much better off. He must be able to throw overhand, under-hand, or sidearm, hard and fast. He must be a sure catch of pop flies [balls under-cut by the batter and popped into the air]. He must catch popups anywhere from the stands behind third, through short left field to the area behind second base.

"His position makes him best suited to be the team's general in charge of defense. He should be the spark plug of his team. He should be a holler guy who keeps his team fired up."

A baseball team may or may not have a field captain. If it does have one, he is often the shortstop. Whether he is captain or not, the shortstop needs leadership ability.

1. Expect every pitched ball to be hit to you. Know what you are going to do with the ball and be sure that you *will* field it.

2. Study the batters. Move right or left according to where the batter most often hits.

3. Be ready to cover third base when the third baseman handles a bunt.

4. Be ready for throws that pass the pitcher when men are on base.

5. Warn your pitcher not to deliver his pitch until you are back in position after feinting at a base runner.

6. Before the play, think of what *might* happen and be prepared.

COVER THIRD BASE WHEN THIRD BASEMAN HANDLES A BUNT

WARN YOUR PITCHER NOT TO DELIVER PITCH UNTIL YOU ARE BACK IN POSITION

8.

PLAYING THIRD BASE

A THIRD baseman handles the ball mainly in two situations. He takes throws made
to third base. He fields any ball he can
reach that is batted into his territory. This
is the area from the left foul line to whatever distance to his left he can go. In addi-
tion, he must field pop fouls between his
territory and the stands.

Third base is referred to by ballplayers
as "the hot corner." This is no joke. A
right-handed batter who rips the ball down
third base way puts the power of his full
swing behind it. A ball sliced toward third
base by a left-handed batter may slant off
the bat very sharply.

If it is not a hot drive of this kind, the
ball is likely to be twisting, spinning,
squirming, hard to handle, or a bunt that
rolls with teasing slowness along the base

70

path. The player guarding the hot corner has no bed of roses.

Third basemen seldom have as many balls hit their way as shortstops or second basemen. Right-handed batters do not often pull the ball sharply enough to hit toward third. Left-handed batters are much more likely to hit away from third base. It is mainly when they are fooled by a pitch and swing too late, or slice an outside pitch, that they hit to third-base territory.

Most balls hit to third get there so quickly that a third baseman can make almost-errors and still have time to throw the batter out at first base. A third baseman doesn't cover as much territory as shortstop or second baseman. Therefore he may be slower of foot.

Almost any third baseman would give you an argument if you said the hot corner was easy to play. It is true that at third base a player gets fewer fielding chances than other infielders, but he is expected to add to the team's batting strength. If he is a

72 power hitter who can provide the long ball, he may play the game a long time. This is possible even if he is slow of foot and a weak fielder. However, a third baseman who is also a good infielder is of much more value to his team. Third basemen with poor fielding skills need to work hard to improve them.

A third baseman should protect about eighteen feet to his left and twelve feet to his right. The farther he can play from the foul line and still move over to grab balls batted near the line, the smaller the hole between shortstop and third baseman.

The third baseman able to protect the foul line and yet narrow the hole is a big asset to his team. When balls batted down the line get past the third baseman they usually go for more than one base. Pitchers appreciate third basemen who can get to such drives and knock them down so that the batter is held to one base.

One of the most difficult plays a third baseman is called on to make is fielding a

swinging bunt. A swinging bunt is not
really a bunt. It is a pitched ball at which
a batter took a full swing but swung a little
too high. The overcut ball trickles over the
grass with no more speed than a bunt. It
usually has a lot of twisting spin. The third
baseman is not expecting a bunt and is
playing deep. For this reason he does not
get a good jump on the ball.

There is only one way to play a swinging bunt with any hope of throwing out
the batter. Charge in and grab the ball
barehanded. Almost in the same motion
of grabbing the ball, snap a throw to the
first baseman.

74   Keep your eye on the ball! Baseball coaches constantly call out this advice. Never is it more necessary than when a third baseman fields a swinging bunt. If he misses his grab for the ball, it may be because he took his eye off the ball and lifted his head too soon.

Third basemen should practice and practice until they are sure death on pop flies. A good third baseman gives any pop fly hit into his territory a tough battle. Perhaps a ball that seems headed into the stands or over the fence will be held back by the wind. You look very foolish if you don't go after a pop fly and the ball falls where you could have caught it.

When you smother those popups, you are helping your pitcher. Go over and catch pop flies hit into the pitcher's territory. He is, first of all, a thrower. As third baseman, you are supposed to be more sure of catching a pop fly than the pitcher is.

Today most teams play for the big inning—a cluster of runs. Playing for one

run is scorned. Teams swing for the fences
and try to knock the ball out of the park.
They do not often use the sacrifice bunt.
Nevertheless a third baseman must be prepared to field bunts coming his way.

With a base runner on third and less
than two out, a third baseman must be on
the alert for a possible squeeze play. In a
play of this kind there is a signal between
the batter and runner as to which pitch the
batter will bunt. The runner dashes for
home plate. The batter bunts the ball.

A squeeze play is difficult to break up.
The third baseman must grab the ball
cleanly and get it to the catcher very fast.
Should a squeeze bunt catch him way back
and unprepared, he has no chance of
breaking it up.

At every pitch, a third baseman must be
alert and on his toes. Let a smart batter see
that the third baseman is asleep and he
may bunt toward third even with two out.

"SQUEEZE PLAY"

THIRD BASEMAN   RUNNER   BATTER

BRIEF TIPS FOR THIRD BASEMEN

1. Practice catching pop flies wherever you can reach them.
2. Be prepared for a possible bunt, especially when there is danger of a squeeze play.
3. When the batter is left-handed, play toward the plate a little more. A left-handed batter can more easily push a bunt your way.
4. When a runner on third tags up on a fly to the outfield, point at his foot. Until the ball touches the fielder's glove he cannot dash for home. When he sees you pointing, he will be especially careful to keep contact with the bag. The fraction of a second he loses in getting away may be just enough added time for the throw to nip him at the plate.

9.
PITCHING

THE pitcher has the ball more often than any other player. His chief role in the game is to pitch the ball in such a way that batters cannot hit it safely far enough and often enough to make more runs than the pitcher's team. Baseball experts say that 75 to 90 per cent of a team's strength is in its pitching. The pitcher has the most exhausting job on a baseball team. He is its first line of defense. With every batter he faces, the pitcher wages a little war.

Control—the ability to throw the ball where you want it—is a pitcher's most important weapon. Until you have control don't play around with fancy pitches. Curve, screwball, slider, knuckler—none of these are of first importance. A pitcher who can throw his fast ball where he wants and when he wants is a better pitcher than one with all kinds of fancy pitches which he can't throw in the strike zone. Practice, *practice*, PRACTICE your control.

Next in importance to control is a good understanding of hitting. A pitcher must study each player's way of batting. The more he himself knows about hitting, the better able he is to pitch to the strengths and weaknesses of batters.

Since the catcher is the one who gives the sign for the pitch, the pitcher needs to have confidence in him. At the same time, he must never forget that catchers are human and can make mistakes. If the wrong kind of pitch is made and the batter blasts the ball, it is the pitcher, not the catcher, who is blamed.

The smart pitcher studies batters constantly. He remembers the type of pitch a batter hits well and what type gives him trouble. Perhaps the catcher's sign is for a pitch that the batter has hit hard before. The pitcher shakes off the sign—usually by wiggling his glove. Then the catcher

will sign for another pitch, or perhaps he
will call time and come out to talk to the
pitcher. Unless the manager has signaled
for a particular pitch, the catcher does not
insist on one. He and the pitcher talk it
over. Both want a pitch that will fool the
batter.

Beginning with his first throw as a
pitcher, a boy should try to make his basic
pitching motion smooth and natural.
There may be a few pitchers with natural
sidearm or underhand delivery. If you
have one of these rare natural motions,
don't allow anyone to change it. Most
young pitchers have a natural three-
quarter overhand style. Whatever his style
of throw, the pitcher must always remember that the main thing is control over his
pitches.

Here is one way to develop control. Take
a piece of canvas or any other kind of cloth
you can get. Paint lines on it to mark the
strike zone. Remember that the strike zone
is a rectangle of space the width of home

80 plate (seventeen inches), extending from the height of the batter's knees up to his armpits. Make a frame for your cloth strike zone by nailing four boards together in a rectangle of this size. Fasten the cloth securely to the frame. Then cut holes about three times as big as a baseball in the corners of it.

Now pitch to it from the pitching distance you are using. If your muscles are still developing, this distance should be less than the regulation sixty feet and six inches, remember. Throw for the holes.

Try fifty throws aimed at the high outside hole. Keep a score of the number of
times the ball goes through. Pitch fifty to
the low inside hole. Keep score. Do the
same for the high inside and low outside
holes. Practice of this type in pitching to
definite spots is bound to improve your
control. Just be careful not to keep at it
each time long enough to risk straining
your arm.

Learn to follow through. It is important
to get the full power of back and shoulders
behind your delivery. Carrying your hand
and arm on in a follow-through motion
after releasing the ball will help.

82 The pitcher must have one foot in contact with the pitching rubber when he releases the pitch. You must learn for yourself the part of the slab from which you throw most comfortably. Some pitch from one end, some from the other end of the slab, and some from the center. Other pitchers vary their position with left or right-handed batters.

A fast ball is not the only type of delivery a pitcher needs. A slow ball once in a while makes the fast ball seem even faster. Used as a change-up—change of pace—a slow ball throws off the batter's timing. A curve now and then keeps the batter from digging in and swinging from the heels on the fast ball.

How do you hold your fast ball? How do you grip your curve? How do you throw a slider? How do you hold your change-up? Such questions as these are always being asked of pitchers.

Ballplayers refer to the different ways of holding pitches as "fingering." Throw a fast ball with the same natural grip you use in picking up a ball you are going to throw. The forefinger and second finger are on top and the thumb on the bottom. The third and little finger fold naturally against the palm.

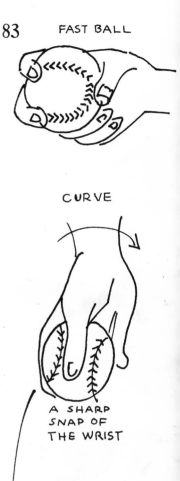

FAST BALL

CURVE

A SHARP
SNAP OF
THE WRIST

The fast ball is delivered straight off the thumb and fingers without twist to right or left. More or less spin is given the ball by the natural release. A good fast ball will rise as it comes to the plate. Ballplayers say that it is "alive" or that there is "a hop on the ball."

Pitchers work until they can deliver a fast ball, a curve, or a change-up with the same pitching motion. The fingering for each pitch is the same. It is the spin given the ball at release which makes the difference.

A curve is pitched with a sharp snap of the wrist outward or down at the instant of release. The ball rolls off the forefinger. It spins toward the first-base side of the plate when a right-handed pitcher throws

84　it. The left-handed pitcher's curve breaks toward the third-base side of the plate.

Young pitchers sometimes speak of having a "drop" or an "outdrop." Professional ballplayers call such pitches "sinkers." The spin of the ball as it rolls over the forefinger at the instant of release determines the type of curve.

Suppose the catcher gives the sign for a change-up pitch. The pitcher grips the ball the same way. He throws it with the same motion. But he lifts the top fingers from the ball as it leaves his hand. A slow curve is pitched with the same wrist snap as the regular curve. But again the top fingers are lifted as the ball is pitched.

You may have heard of a pitch called a "screwball." It is very hard on a pitcher's arm and is difficult to control. Young pitchers will be well advised to stay away from it.

Most pitchers today use a slider. This is fingered like a fast ball but delivered with a slight stiff-wrist twist.

SLIDER

It is a good idea for a pitcher to study the batters constantly. Perfect your control. Stay away from pitches that put extra strain on your arm. Always warm up properly before cutting loose with hard throws. Practice your fielding and try to perfect it. A pitcher who can do this adds a "fifth infielder" to his team's defense.

Back up third base and home on plays where throws are made to those bases. When there are runners on base, break for the plate if a pitch gets away from you and there is a possibility that the ball may get past the catcher.

ON A WILD PITCH THE PITCHER RUNS IN TO COVER HOME PLATE

86 BRIEF TIPS FOR PITCHERS

1. Practice, practice, practice your control.

2. Make batters hit to get on base. Bases on balls can beat you.

3. Bear down on *all* batters. The easy out too often smashes out a vital hit.

4. Practice fielding your position.

5. Study the batters. Use your head, your arm, and every weapon you have in the constant battle with them.

BEARING DOWN

10.
CATCHING

THE catcher is the workhorse of a base-ball team. His role is very important. When his side is in the field he has to be on the alert every second. He must be physically strong and rugged, with a good throwing arm. He needs what players refer to as "baseball savvy" (baseball knowl-edge).

A clever catcher can bring out the best in the pitcher of a team. It is the catcher's job to make the signs which tell the pitcher the kind of pitches to throw. In order to do this, the catcher will study the batter. How does he stand at the plate? Too close? Try curves that break away from him. Does he stand in the front part of the batter's box? Try fast balls.

The catcher notes the way opposing bat-ters swing. He keeps track of how well the

87

batter watches pitches. Does the batter keep his eye on the ball all the way and swing only at pitches in the strike zone? Be careful. He is probably a good hitter. Mix up the pitches. Move the ball around. Keep him off balance. Try not to give him any pitches that are too good.

Does the batter seem overanxious? Is he restless in the box? Give him a slow ball.

Is this batter a guess hitter? Try to give him a pitch that normally would not be thrown in this situation. You have more chance of outguessing him. You may get him to swing at bad pitches.

The catcher makes his mitt a target for his pitcher. He holds the mitt where he wants the pitch. He holds the mitt steady after receiving the ball. This gives the umpire a chance to judge whether the pitch was in the strike zone. You seldom see a top-flight catcher try to pull the ball to one side.

An umpire calls the pitch as he sees it. If the catcher pulls the ball, it is a kind of insult. The catcher is trying to trick the umpire into calling a ball a strike. Would you like that if you were an umpire?

Of course, when you are playing without an umpire, such pulling of the ball leads to endless argument.

The catcher squats in a sitting position to give his sign to the pitcher. His feet are fairly close together at this time. He gives the sign with the fingers of his right hand. His knees prevent it from being seen easily by first- or third-base coach. With his mitt he shields his bare hand from any batter foolish enough to take his eye off the pitcher to peek at the catcher's sign.

To receive the pitch, most catchers take a stance that straddles the plate. That means the feet are eighteen to twenty-one inches apart. Normally the toes will turn

out slightly. The main thing is to assume a stance that will be comfortable.

We said earlier that a simple and commonly used set of signs is: one finger for a fast ball and two fingers for a curve. Wiggling the fingers may be the sign for a slow ball or change-up.

There is no set rule for catchers' signs. If there is any reason to think that rival players are getting them, the signs may be changed from game to game. They may be changed during a game, for that matter.

The catcher may brush his right hand across his right shoulder if he wants the pitch high and outside. He may brush or touch his left shoulder with his mitt for a high pitch inside. Touching the right or left shin guard can be a sign for a pitch low and inside or low and outside, according to which shin is touched.

A catcher should have a strong arm. He must be prepared for attempts to steal bases. Whenever there is a base runner, there is risk of a base-stealing attempt.

In receiving the pitch, the catcher steps forward with his left foot if possible. His pegs to bases are made off the right foot. He cocks his arm and snaps the throw from approximately his right ear.

Few base runners will ever be thrown out by the catcher who uses vital time in taking his arm all the way back to throw. The catcher who takes an extra stride before whipping his peg will not throw many runners out either.

To try to catch without a mask to protect your face would be foolish. The bars of a

catcher's mask interfere with your vision when you are locating a pop fly, however, so you yank off the mask. Now, what to do with it?

Either carry the mask with you until you are under the pop, or fling the mask as far away as you can. A catcher who stumbles over his mask when chasing a foul pop feels foolish. If his team loses a put-out, he will feel even worse.

Experienced catchers turn after foul pops according to the direction of the pitch. Pops fouled from pitches coming to the plate on the glove side will be to the left. Pitches to the bare-hand side will be fouled to the right. After he takes his turn, the catcher throws his head back to locate the ball. If possible, he gets right under the ball as it is coming down. Then he backs up a little in order to catch the ball in front.

Another important part of a catcher's job is to defend the plate when a base runner tries to score. This does not mean simply to straddle the plate and wait. With-

out the ball, you can't possibly put the tag on a runner. Get the ball first. Then block the plate or dive for the runner.

Young catchers will do well to practice footwork. Smooth footwork is as important to a catcher as to a first baseman. The catcher must shift his feet to meet the pitch. A good system of shifting the feet is to make the first step with the foot farthest from the pitch.

Suppose the pitch is wide to the right. Shift the left foot behind the right. Take a wide step with the right foot.

What if the pitch is wide to the left? Shift the right foot behind the left and take a wide stride with the left.

Sometimes pitches are into the dirt. Experienced catchers handle these low pitches by dropping to the knees. Use your body to block the ball if you must. A ball that gets away from the catcher may cost his team a ball game.

94   BRIEF TIPS FOR CATCHERS

1. Make a target with your mitt for your pitcher, and hold it steady.

2. Practice judging and catching pop fouls.

3. Practice getting your mask off when a pop foul is hit. Throw it clear of your path right away or carry it until you locate the ball. In either case there will be less danger of stepping on it.

4. Practice your footwork until you can shift your feet smoothly and automatically on wide pitches.

5. Practice handling bunts near the plate.

6. Study the other team's batters. This is a practice that must go on and on.

IF YOU EXPECT A BUNT, DON'T CROUCH WAY DOWN.. HOLD YOUR MITT A LITTLE HIGHER AND MOVE YOUR RIGHT FOOT BACK SO YOU ARE READY FOR A "QUICK JUMP" ON THE BUNTED BALL

11.
PLAYING THE OUTFIELD

IN general, an outfielder handles the ball only when it is batted into his territory. He may also be called on at times to take a wild throw that gets past an infielder.

According to an old baseball saying, an outfielder ought to pay to get into the park. What is meant, of course, is that these players have very little to do in the field. You would have a hard job finding an out-fielder who would agree.

It is true that an outfielder averages only about three chances per game to field the ball. Nevertheless, he must be as alert and on his toes as any other member of the team. An outfielder covers (patrols) a much larger territory than an infielder. What is more, if he muffs a ball hit into his area, there is no hope of recovering it in time to get the batter out.

96   Outfielders need patience. If you are tense, nervous, or impatient, don't try to play the outfield. Outfielders must expect to wait and wait and wait. Yet they must constantly be on the alert. When the ball finally comes their way, they must be eager to play it.

At every pitch an outfielder rises onto his toes. He has to expect that every hit ball may come to him. What he will do with the ball if it is hit to his field must be always in his mind.

Outfielders and relief pitchers who warm up in the bull pen all through a game have something in common. Although the relief pitcher may never be called to the mound, he throws enough to pitch an entire game. The outfielder may not have a ball batted his way once all through the game. Yet he comes up on his toes and tenses his muscles, ready to start, again and again. During any game, he uses almost enough energy to have fielded every single ball.

Left field, center field, and right field are 97
not all played the same way. Right fielders
protect the right foul line area. They must
play reasonably close to the line. Left
fielders protect the left foul line area and
they too must play fairly close to the line.
This leaves the center fielder with more
ground to cover than either of his teammates. The center fielder needs to be quick
and fast of foot.

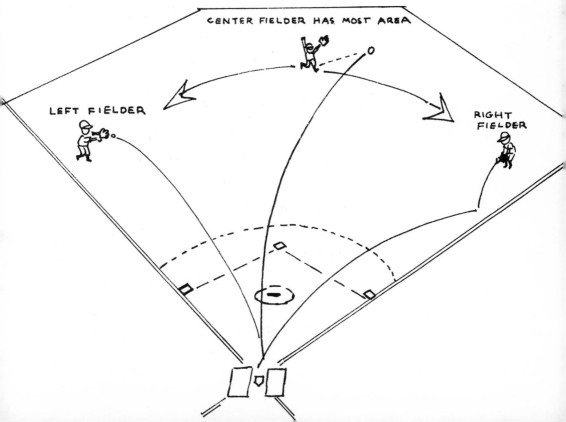

98 Outfielders should practice fielding ground balls as well as catching fly balls and line drives. They must be sure that ground-hit balls do not go past them. A ball that gets past an outfielder almost always allows the batter to stretch his hit for an extra base. The other base runners advance farther than they could have if the ball had not gotten past the outfielder.

Outfielders back up throws made to first, second, and third base. Right fielders back up first base. Center fielders back up second base. Left fielders back up third base.

The late Tris Speaker often talked to young ballplayers. Speaker was, without doubt, one of the greatest fielding outfielders of all time. He is enshrined in the Baseball Hall of Fame. Here is what Tris Speaker said about outfielding:

"Getting the jump on the ball is the most important thing about outfielding. Getting the jump means making a quick start when the ball rides off the bat."

Only with practice can you learn to

judge a hit ball by listening to the crack
of the bat. You must be able to go back
fast for long hits. You must know how to
come in fast for short fly balls. Study the
batters and the type of pitching—fast ball,
curve, or change-up. Pay attention to the
wind and the situation of the game. Learn
to play with all these things in mind.

When you catch the ball, try to be in
position for getting off a throw as soon as
the catch is made. Decide for yourself
whether to attempt a diving catch. Unless
the winning run or tying run is going to
score on a hit, it is probably better to play
safe. Let the ball fall in front where you
can be pretty sure of getting it. A success-
ful diving-circus catch is a great thing to
bring off. If the dive fails, the ball is almost
sure to get past you, and the game may be
lost.

1. DIVING CATCH

2. ROLL OVER

3. BACK ON YOUR FEET

4. GET THAT BALL OFF TO THE INFIELD

An outfielder who catches a ball hit into the air must know where he is going to throw it. The same thing holds true if he fields a grounder or a fly that he could not reach before the ball hit the ground. When there are base runners, the outfielder must get rid of the ball as quickly as possible in order to keep the runners from advancing.

MAN ON SECOND...
TWO OUTS....
SINGLE TO LEFT...
CHARGE BALL
AND FIRE BALL
TO THE PLATE....

BALL
ARRIVES
AT HOME PLATE
ON ONE HOP...
RUNNER SLIDES...
HE'S OUT!

Should an outfielder go after a fly ball
that could also be caught by another fielder,
he is expected to shout, "I'll take it!" If he
feels that another fielder has a better chance
of catching the ball, the outfielder yells,
"You take it!"

Ground balls *must* not get through an
outfielder. If necessary, he should throw
his body on the ball to keep it from going
past him.

We have said that an outfielder must
keep alert and be eager to field balls hit
his way. He must not be too eager, however. It is a good practice to count one
before starting for a line drive. It is far
better to allow the hitter a single than to
start too quickly, misjudge the drive, and
let him stretch the hit to two or three bases
or perhaps a home run.

IT IS
BETTER
TO PLAY
LINER
ON FIRST
BOUNCE
AND HOLD
BATTER
TO A
SINGLE...

BRIEF TIPS FOR OUTFIELDERS

1. Back up the correct base.

2. Think where you will throw the ball if it comes to you.

3. Get rid of the ball as quickly as you can when there are men on the bases.

4. Study opposing batters in order to know where best to play them.

1.

2.

GET
RID OF
BALL
QUICKLY

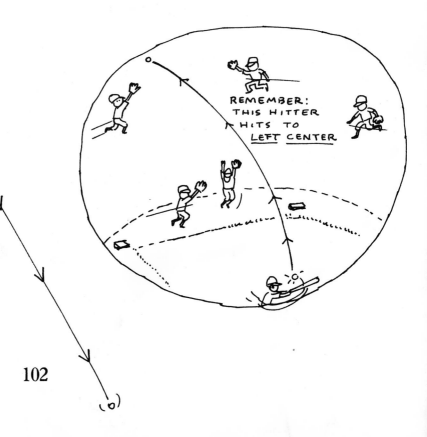

REMEMBER:
THIS HITTER
HITS TO
LEFT CENTER

12.
HITTING AND BASE RUNNING

WE have said that every member of a baseball team has his place in the batting order. When his turn comes up he goes to bat. Even the poorest of batters will sometimes get on base and become a base runner. For this reason hitting and base running concern all ballplayers. To be a good hitter you must win the battle with the pitcher more often than you lose it. This does not mean that you have to hit it safely six or more times out of ten times at bat. It does mean that more times than not you must hit the ball solidly.

Ballplayers say that they "got good wood on the ball," or that they "hit the ball with the fat part of the bat." But the seven teammates behind the pitcher are infielders and outfielders. A batter may win the battle and hit the ball solidly on good wood only

103

to have one of the seven fielders get in front of the drive.

In figuring batting averages, perfect is equal to 1.000. If you batted ten times and made ten safe hits, you would bat 1.000. You would also have every team in baseball anxious to get you.

3 HITS IN 10 AT BAT = .300

Suppose you batted ten times and made three hits. To find your batting average, divide three (the number of hits) by ten (the number of times at bat) and carry the division to three decimal places. Your average would be .300. With .300 or more, you are a very good hitter.

The good hitter has to have a sharp eye and quick, sure reflexes. His timing must be nearly perfect. He needs strength of shoulders, arms, and wrists. These are physical attributes. They can be sharpened and increased by practice, but nature must provide them in the first place. That is why many baseball people say that good hitters are born, not made.

The good hitter must develop judgment and self-confidence. These are qualities which can come through experience.

As for the type and size of bat—which one best fits you? As we said before, this is something you must decide for yourself.

Your swing should be smooth and level, with the bat cutting through the air parallel to the ground. A batter who "chops wood" —swings his bat as he would an ax, with a downward trend—beats the ball into the dirt. His batted balls are likely to be fielded, causing him to be thrown out at first base. The batter who swings with an upward trend undercuts the ball. He is most likely

A WOOD CHOPPER

106 to hit easy fly balls or popups that are camped under by a fielder for put-outs.

Suppose you are up at the plate. As the pitcher begins his delivery motion, you grip your bat. Smoothly and on a level, you bring it forward. Into the swing goes the strength of shoulders, arms, and wrists. As you cock your wrists, step toward the pitcher with the forward foot. Shift your weight to that leg. Keep the leg straight, with the knee firmly set. You will be hitting off the stiff front leg.

KEEP LEG STIFF... KNEE IS FIRMLY SET...

STEP FORWARD

Do not hurry your swing. Only when bat and ball meet should you uncock your wrists. Through wrist snap that adds speed at the moment of contact, you pour power into your swing.

The good hitter keeps his eye on the ball from the moment it leaves the pitcher's hand. There is only a fraction of a second in which to decide whether to swing. He watches the ball as long as possible. Before he swings at it, he wants to be sure the pitch is in the strike zone. He knows that the umpire will call the pitch a ball if it is not in the strike zone. Four balls and he will have a walk—a base on balls. The batter knows that a base on balls often unsettles a pitcher even more than a hit.

The stride is an important part of the swing. The young batter should experiment until he finds the stride exactly right for him. Do not overstride. The overstrider cannot pivot for his follow-through. He is off balance and wastes most of his power. The pitcher is apt to pitch him curves and

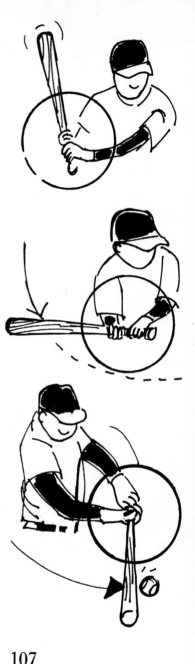

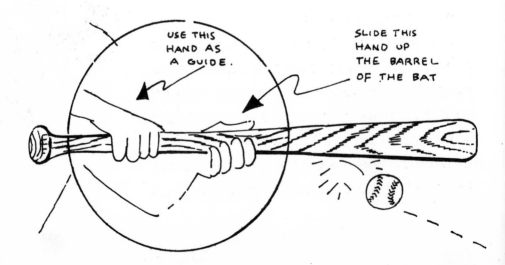

OVERSTRIDER

he will not be in position to step into the ball.

One batting skill that can be—and should be—developed through practice is the bunt. There are times when strategy demands that even a .300 hitter should bunt. The batter shifts his grip on the bat when bunting. He holds the bat loosely and lowers it, parallel to the ground, as the pitcher delivers. He slides his upper hand up the barrel of the bat. His lower hand is used as a guide to get the bat in front of the pitch. The secret of a good bunt is to make the impact of ball and bat as soft as possible.

USE THIS HAND AS A GUIDE.

SLIDE THIS HAND UP THE BARREL OF THE BAT

Of course, the batter knows when he is going to bunt a pitch, but he must keep this a secret from the opposing team. Not until *after* the pitcher delivers does he drop his bat to bunting position.

Getting his safe hits when he is up at the plate is most satisfying to a ballplayer. A good day at the plate erases any memory of "bobbles" (mistakes) in the field. The hitter who has gone "three for four" or "four for four" (made three or four safe hits in four times at bat) feels that everything is right with the world. If the pitcher has given him a hard time, on the other hand, and he has had a bad day at the plate, it may be a good idea to keep away from him for the time being.

When a batter reaches first base without being put out, he becomes a base runner. A speedy, hustling ball club wins games, and good base running adds to its speed, hustle, and aggressiveness. It puts extra pressure on the defense.

Knowing when to run is important, too.

110 This calls for a sharp eye and a good head. Effective base running is much more than just stealing bases.

"If you have fast men on your club," a big league manager said, "use them. Develop the habit in your men of rounding the base on every hit. Have them ready to take that extra base at the slightest opportunity. The other team soon looks for your club to pull a daring play. They get over-anxious. The fielders hurry throws. They try to grab ground balls too quickly and miss the 'handle' on the ball. Soon your men are getting that extra base handed to them on a silver platter."

The good base runner is constantly alert. He knows at all times how many men are out. He keeps an eye on the coaches at first base and third base. He depends on them and obeys their signs. He always watches the runner ahead of him. Nothing makes a base runner look more stupid than for two men to wind up on the same base.

As we said before, in modern baseball

the aim, more often than not, is to play for the big inning—the cluster of runs. Managers are not eager to risk breaking the back of an inning that promises to be big by sending a base runner down to steal. Yet there are times when the steal of a base adds a great deal to the strategy of a ball game.

It is rarely a good idea to attempt a steal with nobody out. A steal is attempted only when there is a chance of an important run, or when a member of the defensive team is not on the alert.

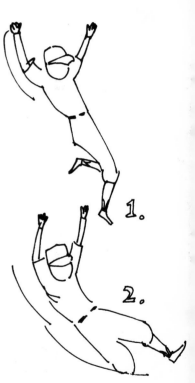

Sliding headfirst is not recommended. There is too much risk of injury. In sliding feet first, there is a choice of two methods. One way is to slide into the bag on the right leg and hook the sack with the left toe. In the other method, the player slides to the side away from the man covering the bag and gives him as small a tag target as possible.

112 Learn to relax and lose any fear you may have about sliding. Practice until it becomes automatic. Wear sliding pads if possible. Once you have started a slide never change your mind. The half slide is a good way of getting hurt.

A slide serves two purposes: (1) It avoids a tag by the baseman. (2) It prevents overrunning the base and being tagged out after the throw has been beaten.

The smartest base runner will sometimes find himself trapped. Don't give up without a battle. Keep the rundown going. A fielder may become overanxious and mishandle the ball. Even though you are eventually out, by jockeying back and forth you give base runners behind you a chance to advance to the farthest base possible.

13.

STRATEGY—OFFENSIVE AND DEFENSIVE

THERE are many strategic moves made in baseball games that help teams win. For a professional club, the manager determines strategy. For a boys' team, strategy is decided on by the coach. In both cases, one of the base coaches relays the signs to batters and base runners.

All teams use a base coach at first base and one at third base. These coaches help base runners by keeping track of the ball. They warn runners when to scurry back. Players who are not likely to come to bat during the inning—or substitute players not in the line-up—serve as coaches. Big-league teams have men who are specialists in coaching, but not all clubs can afford extra coaches.

A big league manager who was asked what qualities were needed by a coach re-

114   plied, "Be smart, sensible, and sharp as a tack. Be a good listener and ready with sound advice. Be able to make decisions right now, and willing to accept the blame if the decision is wrong. Be ready to take advantage of any opening you see. Be willing to accept without protest blame for errors that may not have been yours. Be prepared to get no credit when things turn out right. Own the coolness and ability to direct traffic at the busiest corner of your city. Have all these qualities and you can *try* to be a coach!"

Defensive strategy is fairly cut and dried. The team practices defensive plays which include (1) pick-off plays, (2) cut-off plays, (3) throwing to the proper base, (4) defense against the sacrifice bunt and against the squeeze play, (5) pulling the infielders in on the grass to cut off a possible run at the plate, (6) playing the infield deep and trying to get the double play. The manager or coach makes a sign telling which pattern to use.

It is the offensive strategy that the base coaches direct. They do this by flashing signs to batters and base runners. The sign may tell the player to *hit* or *take* a pitch, to steal or to play it safe. Although coaches may use various sets of signs, these are always kept as simple as possible.

The *take* sign tells the batter not to swing at the upcoming pitch. For this sign, the coach might touch flesh after touching cloth. He might touch cloth after touching flesh, or he might touch flesh after touching flesh. Sometimes the *take* sign is made by one hand or the other touching the letters or club insignia on the shirt front. Coaches have many different ways of flashing this signal to the players.

The *hit* sign which gives the batter the manager's approval to swing at the upcoming pitch may be any of those or something altogether different.

Next time you watch a ball game keep your eye on the base coaches. One of them —or both—will make dozens of different

116   motions. If you didn't know that the motions were made for a purpose, you might think the coach had a nervous ailment that made him jumpy. A few of the many motions carry a message—give a sign. The other motions are meaningless. Opponents are constantly watching. If they can discover the signs the other team uses, you can see what a big advantage this gives them. By making many, many motions, the coaches hope to confuse their opponents.

For base runners, however, coaches do use certain definite signs. Swinging a hand inward toward the chest tells the runner to keep coming. Pushing the hands away from the body with palms outward orders the runner to stop, to hold back. Lifting the arms above the head means that there is no need to slide. Holding the hands parallel to the ground with palms down is the sign for the runner to slide or "hit the dirt."

It is the third-base coach's responsibility to send a runner home or hold him at third. It is the coach who decides whether a fly ball is hit deeply enough for the runner to risk tagging up and dashing for the plate after the catch. If he decides to send the runner home, the coach stands as close to the runner as the boundary of the coaching box allows.

The runner tags up. He pays no attention to the third baseman, who is probably pointing at his foot. He pays no attention to the ball out in the field. A bare instant before the ball contacts the fielder's glove, the coach yells, "Go!" He is not trying to cheat. He knows that the runner cannot legally take off before the ball strikes the fielder's glove. But the coach yells the starting signal because he knows that by the time the runner's reflexes are set in motion, the ball will have hit the fielder's glove.

Casey Stengel, who managed the New York Yankees to more World Series titles than any other manager, could add a lot more to the bit of strategy outlined here. Learning about baseball is something that can go on and on.

14.
KEEPING SCORE

SCOREKEEPERS may have little differences in the way they keep score, but there are certain things that are done alike.

Positions in the field are numbered. Pitcher is Number 1. Catcher is Number 2. First base is Number 3. Second base is Number 4. Third base is Number 5. Shortstop is Number 6. Starting in left field, the outfield positions are numbered 7, 8, 9.

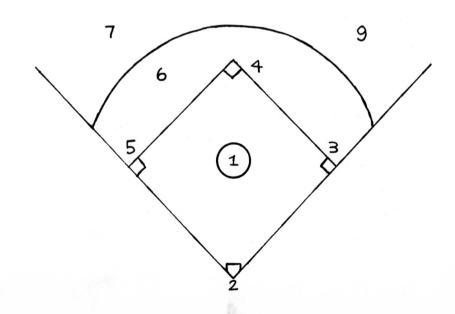

A score card has squares for each inning
for each player in the batting order. This
is the way a score card looks before being
used.

PLAYER	1	2	3	4	5	6	7	8	9

Let's score the inning that our make-
believe teams played way back in Chapter
4 of the book.

White, the leadoff man in the top of the
first inning, struck out. Practically all
scorers show a strike-out with a K. So we

120   will show that White struck out by putting a K in the square opposite his name.

Tomson was the second batter. His little blooper fly to left field fell safely. To show that he reached first base we make a line straight up and down in the right side of his square. Above this vertical line we make a shorter line slanting upward toward the left. This shows that he reached first base on a hit which went to the left side of the diamond.

Loomis was the name of the third batter in the top of the inning. Loomis received a base on balls. Some scorers make two small B's in the upper right-hand corner to stand for "base on balls." Our system is to use a vertical line to show that Loomis reached first base and then to place a small w (walk) at the upper right. We also make a horizontal line in Tomson's square because he reached second base—halfway to completing his square—when Loomis was given a base on balls.

Do you remember what Jones, the third

batter, did? He hit a sharp ground ball that skipped a little to the shortstop's right. The ball was fielded cleanly and the shortstop tossed to the second baseman. Loomis was forced out. The second baseman threw hard and quickly to first base. The ball arrived before Jones could touch the bag and Jones was out, too.

This action is shown on the scorecard by making a 6-4 in Loomis' square. This shows that shortstop—Number 6—threw to the second baseman—Number 4—for the put-out. In the square opposite Jones we write 4-3. This indicates that Number 4 (second baseman) threw to Number 3 (first baseman) to retire Jones.

The home team in our make-believe game had its shortstop, Smith, leading off. Smith hit a pitch solidly on the good wood of his bat. But, remember, it went on a line straight at the left fielder. We show the action in Smith's square by L-7, lined out to left field.

The second batter in the bottom of the

inning was Johnson, right fielder, who bats left-handed. The pitcher threw him curves until the count was one and two. Then a fast ball pitched too far inside hit the batter on the arm.

We make a vertical mark in Johnson's square. Then to indicate how he reached base, we make a small HB (for "hit batsman") in the upper right corner.

Our third batter was the center fielder, Speed. He is very fast and an excellent bunter. His bunt was so good that neither the first baseman nor the pitcher could field the ball in time to throw him out. It was a hit. We add a mark at right angles to the vertical line in Johnson's square to show that he moved to second base. We make a vertical line in the right portion of Speed's square to show that he reached first base. We make a little slanting line in the upper right corner to show that the hit went to the right side of the diamond.

The fourth batter was Parks, a third baseman who often hits a long ball. This

ONE-HOPPER TO PITCHER ·· WHO THROWS RUNNER OUT!

time his long ball was caught by the center fielder for the second out. It is shown by F-8.

Next, Modjewski, tall and husky first baseman, came to the plate. Modjewski swung mightily but topped a one-hopper to the pitcher and was thrown out at first to retire the side. Modjewski's out is shown on the scorecard 1-3, which indicates that Number 1 (pitcher) fielded a grounder off his bat and threw to Number 3 (first baseman), who made the put-out.

123

This is the way the score card would look for top and bottom of the first inning.

TOP

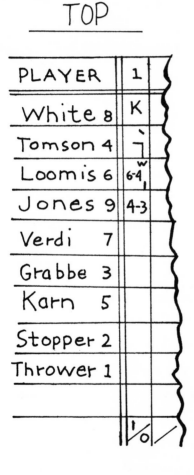

PLAYER	1
White 8	K
Tomson 4	↘
Loomis 6	6-4 (w)
Jones 9	4-3
Verdi 7	
Grabbe 3	
Karn 5	
Stopper 2	
Thrower 1	

BOTTOM

PLAYER	1
Smith 6	L-7
Johnson 9	HB ↘
Speed 8	
Parks 5	F-8
Modjewski 3	1-3
Maxon 7	
Down 4	
Receivo 2	
Hurler 1	

Umpires are important in a baseball game. They do not wear a uniform as the players do. Usually, however, umpires dress alike in dark trousers and coats, or dark shirts.

The umpire-in-chief stands behind the catcher. He rules on whether pitches are strikes or balls. If the ball crosses any part of the plate in the strike zone, the umpire calls it a strike. If the pitch is wide, too close to the batter, higher or lower than the strike zone, the umpire calls it a ball.

STRIKES

BALLS

Umpires use the right hand to signal strikes and the left hand to signal balls. There is no set rule as to what motion shall be made. Some umpires merely point a finger toward the ground. Others are more dramatic, especially in the case of a third strike, when they may put the whole body into the act.

SAFE

OUT

Base umpires signal that a runner is safe by spreading or swinging their hands in a plane parallel to the ground. A put-out of a base runner is indicated by jerking the right thumb over the shoulder. Again, there is no set rule. Some umpires use a push-pull gesture of the right fist to make the *out* sign.

126

To include everything that could be said
about baseball would fill a gigantic book.
Many points have not even been men-
tioned. As we said before, however, learning about baseball is a process you can go
on and on with, once you have started. In
the pages that follow you will find some of
the more common baseball terms.

BASEBALL TERMS

Alive or Live—The ball is alive when legally in play. Ballplayers speak of a pitcher's fast ball being alive or live when it hops and moves.

At Bat—When a player is at the plate to take his turn at hitting or when a whole team is in for its half of the inning on the offensive.

Baseball Hall of Fame—A center at Cooperstown, New York (generally regarded as the birthplace of baseball). On display are plaques commemorating famous ballplayers, uniforms worn by some of the stars, and bats and balls used when outstanding records were made.

Base Hit—When a batted ball is fair, and no error is made, and the batter reaches base safely.

128

Base on Balls—Awarded to a batter to whom four pitches out of the strike zone are made before he bats a fair ball or takes three strikes.

Base Runner—A player who reaches base safely becomes a base runner.

Batted Out of the Box—When a pitcher is taken from the game because the opposing batters are making too many hits.

Batter—The player at bat.

Big Inning—An inning in which a team scores several runs.

Bottom of an Inning—The half of an inning when the home team is at bat. Sometimes called the last of the inning.

Box Scores—Records of baseball games compiled from score cards. Box scores appear on sports pages daily during the baseball season.

Bull Pen—The area where relief pitchers warm up during the game.

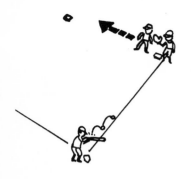

Bunt Situation—A time when it is good strategy for the team at bat to try a bunt. Example: A runner is on first base; nobody is out; your team is a run behind, or the score is tied. You want to move the base runner to second so that he will be in position to score on a base hit.

Camp Under—The term used when any fielder reaches a fly ball and waits to catch it.

Catcher—The player who wears mask, chest protector, shin guards, and big mitt and stands behind the plate to receive pitches. He is Number 2 on the score card.

Center Field—The outfield area behind second base to the outfield barrier and stretching between left field and right field.

Center Fielder—The player who guards center field against batted balls. He is Number 8 on the score card.

Change of Pace, or Change-Up—A pitch

used to vary fast ball pitching. The
pitcher lets up on his grip and the ball
leaves his hand with less speed than
usual.

Class D—The lowest rank among professional baseball leagues.

Count—The balls and strikes on a batter at any given time. The number of strikes comes last. Example: For two strikes and three balls, the count is three and two.

Curve—A pitched ball that moves to right or left or downward just before it reaches the plate, or as it crosses the plate.

Dead Ball—The name given to the ball when it is not legally in play.

Diamond—The infield of a baseball playing area containing home plate, first base, second base, and third base.

Digging In—When a batter sets his spikes firmly in the batter's box, prepared to swing with all his power.

Double—A base hit on which the hitter reaches second base without a fielding error being made on the play. A two-base hit.

Double Play—Two put-outs made on one continuous play.

Double Steal—When base runners on first and second—or second and third—or first and third—successfully advance without the ball's being hit or the batter's being awarded a base on balls.

Drag Bunt—A bunt made when the batter is in motion from the plate so that he drags the ball part way along with him.

Dugout—The dug-out area where a team's bench is located, usually near the stands behind first base or third base.

132

Error—A misplay of the ball that allows
a batter to reach base safely or advance
one or more bases.

Fair Ball—A legally batted ball that settles
on ground—or passes through the air—
between the first base line and the third
base line; also a ball batted to the outfield which first touches ground between
foul lines or is touched by a player while
between the lines.

Fast Ball—A pitch thrown with great
speed.

Fielder's Choice—A fielder's decision to
make a play to put out any base runner
rather than the batter. The batter might
reach base safely but would not deserve
credit for a base hit. Usually indicated
on the score card by an FC in the batter's
square.

Fingering—The way a pitcher holds the
ball for a particular type of pitch.

FLY
BALL

134   *First Base*—The base at the corner of the
diamond to the right of home plate.

First Baseman—The player who fields the
first-base position. He is Number 3 on
the score card.

Fly Ball—A batted ball that is higher in
the air than a line drive.

Follow-Through—The continuing motion
of arm, shoulder, and body after a
thrown ball has left the hand or after the
bat has been swung over the plate.

Force Play—A base runner must leave his
base because another runner behind him
is entitled to the base. Hence the first
runner is forced to advance.

Foul Ball—A batted ball which is not a
fair ball.

Foul Lines—The lines extending from the
back corner of home plate, past first base
and third base.

Foul Pop or Popup—A batted ball popped into the air in foul territory.

Get the Two—Make a double play.

Good Wood—The fat part of the bat.

Grounder—A batted ball on the ground.

Ground Rules—Special rules used when the distances from base line to stands, or from home plate to the outfield barriers down the foul lines, are less than those recommended by the official rules.

Guess Hitter—A batter who thinks he knows what type of pitch is coming.

Hill—The raised pitching area.

Hit—See *Base Hit*.

Hit to Get On—The words fielders sometimes shout when they want the pitcher to force the batter to hit to get on base, thus giving them a chance to get him out.   135

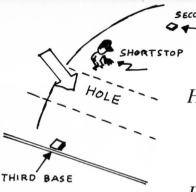

SECOND BASE

SHORTSTOP

HOLE

THIRD BASE

Hole—The area between shortstop and third baseman which is hardest for either to guard against batted balls.

Home Base—Home plate.

Home Run—A hit that enables the batter to travel safely all the way around the four bases.

Hop on the Ball—A fast ball that rises and hops just before reaching the plate.

Hurler—The pitcher.

Infield—That part of a baseball playing area within the diamond.

Infielder—A first baseman, second baseman, shortstop, or third baseman.

Inning—The division of a baseball game completed when both teams have had a time at bat.

136

In on the Grass—Applied to infielders
when they move to the edge of the grass
in front of the base paths between first
and second, and second and third, hop-
ing to field any ground-hit ball in time
to make a play at the plate to cut off a
run. This happens only when there is a
base-runner on third and less than two
outs.

Inside Baseball—The strategy of the game.
Playing the percentages and using steals,
bunts, and any plays that are not merely
mechanical and may help a team win.

In the Dirt—Any thrown ball, pitch, or
peg to a base, so low that it hits the
ground before reaching the receiver.

In the Field—When the players of a team
are in fielding position while the other
team bats.

138 *Knocked off the Hill*—An expression used when a pitcher is removed from the game because batters have been hitting his delivered balls too often and too hard.

Leadoff Man—The player who bats first in batting order, or who leads off an inning.

Left Field—The outfield area behind third base and shortstop to the outfield barrier and stretching from left foul line to center field.

Left Fielder—The player responsible for fielding batted balls into the left-field area. He is Number 7 on the score card.

Line Drive—A hit ball that is off the ground but not high or looping.

Long Ball—A long drive good for two or more bases. A ball hit so deeply into the outfield that base runners may advance after the catch.

Make a Target—When a fielder gives the
thrower something to aim at. Example:
When a catcher holds up his mitt to give
pitcher or infielders an aiming point.

Out—One of the required retirements to
end a team's at-bat portion of an inning.

Outfield—That part of a baseball playing
area from the infield to the outer barrier.

Outfielder—A player responsible for left
field, center field, or right field.

Passed Ball—A pitched ball that gets away
from the catcher.

Pegs—Throws by the catcher to any base
or throws by an infielder to a base when
the aim is to cut down a base runner.

Pick-Off Play—A play in which pitcher
and shortstop—or second baseman—co-
operate to get out a runner leading off
second base.

Pinch Hitter—A batter sent to the plate
to bat for a weaker hitter.

140 *Pitched Ball*—A ball legally delivered from the pitcher to home plate.

Pitcher—The player who pitches to rival batters from the pitcher's rubber. He is Number 1 on the score card.

Pitchout—A ball deliberately pitched out of the strike zone. The catcher signs for a pitchout when he thinks a base runner will try a steal or when he thinks the hit-and-run sign has been given by the team at bat.

Pivot Man—Shortstop or second baseman, whichever takes the throw at second base on double-play tries.

Playing It Safe—When a base runner hugs the bag and takes no chances of being caught out.

Popup—A ball undercut by the batter so that it goes into the air upward, making it easy to catch.

Pull—To get the bat around so fast that contact with the ball is made in front of the plate. Right-handed pull hitters drive with power to left field. Left-handed pull hitters have most power to right field.

Punch the Ball—Punch the bat in front of the pitched ball instead of taking a full swing.

Put-Out—When a player is called out by the umpire for any reason.

Putting the Tag On—The catcher or any infielder who covers a base, gets the ball, and tags the base runner with it.

RBI—Runs batted in.

Relief Pitcher—A pitcher who comes in from the bull pen to take over when the regular pitcher is forced to leave the game for any reason.

Rhubarb—An argument, usually involving several players and the umpires.

142   *Right Field*—The part of the outfield area from center field to the right foul line.

Right Fielder—The player who fields the right field position. He is Number 9 on the score card.

Rubber—The pitching slab.

Rundown—When a base runner is trapped between bases with fielders trying to get him out.

Runs—When a player has legally progressed around the bases without being put out.

Sack—Another name for first, second, or third base.

Sacrifice Bunt—A bunt on which the batter is thrown out at first, but any runners on base advance.

Sacrifice Fly—A fly ball hit deeply enough into the outfield so that a runner on third can safely score after the catch.

Sand-Lot Ball—Baseball played without coaching or organized supervision, but not necessarily played on a sand lot.

Scouts—Men employed by major-league clubs to search for baseball talent. Part-time scouts, sometimes called "bird dogs," point out to regular scouts boys who may show promise.

Second Base—The base at the corner of the diamond opposite home plate. Sometimes called the keystone sack.

Second Baseman—The player responsible for fielding balls hit into the second-base area. He is Number 4 on the score card.

Shelled off the Mound—When a pitcher is hit so hard that he gives way to a relief pitcher. Also referred to as "knocked out of the box" or "batted off the hill."

Shortstop—The area of the infield between second base and the third baseman's territory. The player who fields this area. He is Number 6 on the score card.

144 *Shutout*—A game in which the rival team fails to score a run.

Signal—Sign. It may be given by any player or flashed to coaches by managers on the bench and then relayed to players. A sign can be a word or gesture—whatever is agreed on beforehand to have a certain meaning.

Single—A base hit good for one base.

Sinker—A curve that breaks downward.

Slab—The pitching rubber.

Slider—A pitch that comes up to the plate like a curve, then slides or spins.

Slow Ball—A pitch delivered with much less speed than other pitches. Used as a change-up.

Slump—A word used to describe situations in which a batter, pitcher, or fielder is doing poorly, or when a whole team has a losing streak.

Southpaw—A left-handed pitcher.

Squeeze Bunt—The bunt in a squeeze play.

Squeeze Play—A play intended to score a runner from third base by having the batter bunt while the runner dashes headlong for the plate. Runner and batter know from signs which pitch is going to be bunted.

Steal (second, third, home)—When a batter advances a base by beating the defensive effort to throw him out and the play does not involve a batted ball.

Strawberries—Term used to describe the scraped areas on hips or legs that often result from sliding without pads.

Strike Zone—The area over the plate, above the batter's knees and below his armpits.

Swing for the Fences—Swing with plenty of power, trying to knock the ball over the fence.

146 *Swinging Bunt*—A bunt made when a batter takes a full swing at a pitched ball but tops it, causing a slow roller.

Tagging—Touching a base runner with the ball.

Tag Up—A base runner ready to make a try for the next base, keeps one foot in contact with the bag until a fly ball touches the fielder's glove.

Take—The sign a coach gives a batter when he is not to offer at the next pitch.

Taking a Throw—When a baseman receives the peg from another player.

Third Base—The bag at the left corner of the diamond.

Third Baseman—The player who guards the third-base area against batted balls and covers the bag. He is Number 5 on the score card.

Top of an Inning—When the visiting team is at bat.

Triple—A three-base hit—one that allows the batter to reach third base.

Triple Play—Three put-outs made in the same continuous play. It rarely happens.

Umpire—An official in a baseball game who calls plays at the bases, and balls and strikes at the plate.

Visiting Team—The team that bats first.

Wild Pitch—A pitch so wide, high, or low that the ball cannot be handled by the catcher. This is a battery error charged against the pitcher. Neither a wild pitch nor a passed ball has any meaning unless there are runners on base. Otherwise a wild pitch is usually ruled a ball.

Wrong Field—A right-handed batter's hitting to right field, or a left-handed batter's hitting to left field.

INDEX

148

About the Author

C. Paul Jackson's interest in boys and in sports has been demonstrated in his coaching, his teaching, and his writing. For many years, Mr. Jackson was on the faculty of the Lincoln Junior High School in Kalamazoo and officiated at athletic contests in Southwestern Michigan schools. He is the author of *Little Leaguer's First Uniform, Rose Bowl All-American,* and *Spice's Football.*

Mr. Jackson received his A.B. degree and teaching certificate from Western Michigan College of Education and an M.A. degree from the University of Michigan.

About the Illustrator

Leonard Kessler is an illustrator of children's books as well as a designer and commercial artist. He was born in Akron, Ohio, but moved to Pittsburgh with his family when he was quite young. He has a degree in fine arts, painting, and design from the Carnegie Institute of Technology in Pittsburgh. Mr. Kessler and his wife, Ethel, who is a writer of children's books, and their two children live in New City, New York.